The Complete Book of Tanning Skins and Furs

James E. Churchill

Stackpole Books

Published by
STACKPOLE BOOKS
Cameron and Kelker Streets
P. O. Box 1831
Harrisburg, PA 17105

Printed in the U.S.A.

Library of Congress Cataloging in Publication Data

Churchill, James E., 1934-
  The complete book of tanning skins and furs.

  Includes index.
  1. Tanning. I. Title.
TS965.C55   1983   675'.23   83-9151
ISBN 0-8117-1719-4

Contents

1 Introduction to Tanning   1
    Procedures, Tools, and Materials

2 Tanning Small Animal Skins:Beginning Projects   13
    Squirrel and Raccoon

3 Tanning Small Furbearers   24
    Muskrat, Weasel, Skunk, Mink, and Rabbit

4 Making Buckskin   42

5 Tanning the Large Furbearers   56
    Fox, Coyote, Otter, Fisher, Beaver, and Raccoon

6 Tanning Moose and Elk Hides   75

7 Tan Your Own Bearskin Rug   85

8 Tanning Thin Domestic Animal Skins   100
     Sheep, Goat, Calf, and Pig

9 Tanning Thick Domestic Hides For Rugs,
   Robes, or Leather   115
     Horse and Cow

10 Tanning Reptile, Fish, and Bird Skins   129
     Alligator, Fish, Snake, Frog, Lizard, and Bird

11 Making Your Own Tanning Tools   143

12 Primitive Tanning Methods   160
     History, Traditional Methods, and Projects

13 Using Your Leather   169
     Grades, Tools, and Projects for Leather Working

14 Solutions and Formulas   180

   Glossary   190

   Index   193

Introduction To Tanning

Tanning is the science and art of turning perishable animal skins into leather and furs. This age-old process can yield a luxurious fur garment or an indispensable leather item, and no artificial product to this day can replace or duplicate the properties of a tanned hide.

A hide is the outer tissue of an animal body made up of once-living cells and their products. Tanning a skin involves removing the tissues which cannot be converted into leather and the treatment of the other tissues so they won't rot and will stay flexible and strong.

GENERAL TANNING PROCEDURES FOR FUR AND LEATHER

Skinning the Animal

The actual tanning process begins with the obtaining of a skin. When a domestic animal skin is being tanned, the beast is slaughtered and skinned before the body heat leaves the tissues. This can be done by the tanner himself, but domestic skins can be easily and inexpensively obtained at a slaughterhouse or farm. When choosing a skin to buy, remember that tanning accentuates any defects or holes in a skin; therefore, good leather cannot be made from a damaged or poorly handled skin, although inconsequential holes in the hide can be sewn up.

Wild animals are hunted or trapped and, as with domestic animals, they are best skinned while the body is still warm. Industrial tanners say that a skin is as perishable as the meat, so the sooner the skin is removed from an animal and salted or dried, the higher the leather quality will be.

The two skinning methods used in this book are open skinning and case skinning. In the discussion of each individual animal, the skinning method is specified; but as a general rule, large domestic animals are open skinned and smaller furbearers are case skinned.

To open skin an animal, a knife cut is made up the belly from anus to lower lip, and then the cut is extended up the inside of each leg to the hoof. Using a knife and your fingers, carefully remove the skin from the belly to the back so it lays flat when you are done.

Most smaller animals are case skinned, which leaves the skin more or less whole. A cut extending from one hoof to the other on the inside of the back legs opens the animal skin from the bottom. The skin is then removed from the back legs upward, turning it inside out as you progress up the body toward the head. The head is skinned out last. Case skinned hides are shaped like a tapered tube or bag.

Salting the Hide

After the large pieces of flesh and fat have been removed from the skin with a knife (see fleshing section for details), the skin can be tanned immediately or it can be salted or frozen. If you wish to begin the tanning process at this point, the relaxing or soaking stage begins here and salting is not necessary.

However, if you wish to keep the hide in this "raw" or "green" state for any period of time at all, it must be preserved in some way or it will decompose just as any other part of the animal would. If it is double wrapped and folded so that the skin side is in, a hide can be frozen in a freezer for up to one year and then thawed and tanned.

Another method of preservation is salting the hide. The fresh hide is first washed in warm, soapy water and carefully cleaned to remove all blood and dirt. Rinse the hide thoroughly in clean, warm water, try to shake out the excess moisture, and tack it or fit it onto a stretching board or frame until it is damp dry.

Once the skin is removed from the stretching board, it can be salted. Using two cups of salt for every pound of hide, pour the salt on the flesh side of the skin and rub it in. Be sure to thoroughly salt the entire skin, paying attention to the edges and the eye, ear, and nose areas. Roll the skin up flesh side in, and place it on a board that has one end slightly inclined so that any moisture can drain away from the skin.

After thirty-six hours, unroll the hide, scrape off the old salt, and resalt it using two cups of salt for each pound of hide. Reroll the skin and replace it on the board; after forty-eight hours, unroll the skin, hang it up by the nose, and allow it to dry away from sunlight or artificial heat. You now have a salted hide that will remain preserved for up to six months if protected from predators such as bugs and rodents.

Soaking the Skin

Before the tanning process can begin, a skin must be soaked to relax and soften it. A fresh skin should immediately be placed in a saltwater bath if it is to be tanned immediately rather than preserved. This bath removes body heat, dissolves proteins that hinder the tanning solution, loosens and softens the flesh and fat left on the skin, and opens the pores of the skin for better penetration of the tanning solution.

In the case of a frozen, unsalted skin, after it is slowly thawed, it is also soaked in the saltwater bath. This bath has the same benefits for a frozen skin as it has for a fresh skin.

Warning: As soon as a skin that will be tanned with the hair or fur left on has soaked long enough to be limp, it should immediately be removed from the water and the hair side of the skin dried by toweling and brushing or by directing the air from a vacuum cleaner or hair dryer on the fur. Remember that the longer the fur is soaked, the stronger the possibility that the hair will begin to pull out of the skin (which does not make any difference when leather is being made).

Salted skins are stiff and so they also need to be soaked, but great care must be taken in this process since bending or twisting the stiff hide will crack or weaken the leather. If you cannot find a container big enough to accommodate the skin in its hardened state, partially relax the skin by laying it flesh side up and covering it with damp sawdust, kitty litter, or cloths.

When the skin is soft enough to bend, fill a container with a solution made of one teaspoon of household bleach for each five quarts of clean water. Since this skin must be soaked until it is soft, the possibility of hair slippage is increased. If the skin will be tanned with the hair on, use cold water and soak the skin for one hour, then change the water after the first hour. The bleach slows hair slip because it retards the action of the bacteria that cause it. A small amount of ammonia can be added to speed up the penetration of the water, if desired.

If the skin is soft enough to be worked with, put it on the fleshing beam and work over the flesh side of the skin with the back of the fleshing knife or with a serrated knife that will scrape through the outer membrane in several places. This will also cause the water to penetrate faster. Now return the skin to the water and soak it for four more hours or until it is soft. In four hours, if the skin isn't completely relaxed, change the water again. While you are changing the water, you can scrape it again to help soften it. Watch the skin closely and remove it as soon as possible if it will be tanned with the hair on.

If the skin is to be tanned for leather, the water only has to be changed once unless it is very dirty. Extremely dirty skins should be washed in warm water containing bleach and detergent.

There are a few furs with thin skin and long hair, such as the fox, that should never be totally immersed in a soaking water. Instead the skin is released by applying the soak water to the skin side only of the "pelt" (dried fur skin) with a sponge or brush. Another widely used method is to immerse the skin in a container of sawdust that has been dampened with the soak water.

Fleshing the Skin

After the hide is relaxed, it must be fleshed very well to remove all of the meat and fat and the thin membrane (found on some skins) that overlay the true skin. Fleshing can be a very easy task as when fleshing a properly skinned sheepskin, or it can be a wearisome task as when fleshing a dried and rehydrated otter pelt.

Fleshing is usually done by placing the skin hair side down on a hard surface and scraping the flesh side with a fairly sharp blade. It is very easy to cut holes in the skin during this procedure so great care should be taken at first to avoid this error. The beginner should use a fairly dull blade and avoid pushing too hard. Working with a small area of the skin will also help to prevent fleshing cuts or nicks. Extremely fresh skins will not flesh well until they have been salted and cooled. Soaking the skin in the mild alkalis such as washing soda, borax, or ammonia water also softens the tissues and aids in removing the meat and fat if it can't be readily scraped off otherwise. Fleshing beams and different shaped fleshing knives have been developed to help in this work.

Dehairing the Hide

If a skin is to be made into leather or rawhide, it must be dehaired either after it is fleshed or during this process. Dehairing is accomplished by soaking the skin in lime water, lye water, or even water containing wood ashes until the hair slips. The skin is then placed flesh side down on a hard surface, such as a fleshing beam, and the hair is scraped away with a fleshing knife or blade. If the skin is properly prepared, the hair will come off so easily that most of it can be removed by brushing it with the hand. After the hair is scraped away, the fleshing knife is pushed hard against the skin to remove the dirt and lime from the surface, a process called "scudding."

After the skin is dehaired and scudded, it is rinsed very well in clear water, and immersed in a vinegar and water solution to neutralize the lime in the skin. This process, called "bating," is done to neutralize the pH of the skin so the tanning solution, which is acidic, will not be weakened. Fur skins that have been soaked in washing soda or borax also should be bated before they are tanned.

Tanning the Skin

Skins that have been properly fleshed and dehaired are ready to put in the tanning baths. Acid tans or "pickle" tans are widely used either as complete tans, or as pretans for chrome and vegetable tanning. Sulfuric acid and oxalic acid both cure a hide very well and are extremely simple to mix up. Both are mixed in the amount of one ounce or less of pure acid and one pound of salt for each gallon of water and pound of skin. The skin is immersed in these acid baths and soaked until the tannage completely penetrates the skin.

Ammonium alum, potash-alum, and basic aluminum sulfate also are time-honored tanning substances when mixed with salt and dissolved in water for immersion tans. They are widely used for fur skins and robe tanning because they leave the leather relatively soft and white. Both acid and alum tans can be used as "tawing" substances where the tannage is mixed as a paste and applied to the skin side only to avoid any danger of hair slippage or other undesirable result of immersion tanning.

Skins that are acid or alum tanned are more correctly "dressed" than tanned. They have most of the qualities of tanned skins, but if they are soaked or wetted repeatedly they lose their elasticity and can even rot because alum and acid are water soluble and will "leach" away. However, since most skins never come in contact with water because they can be cleaned with dry cleaning fluid or gasoline and sawdust, either tannage will give satisfactory results under most conditions. Skins can also be treated with oil or skin dressing to make them more water resistant.

Hides tanned with acid or alum will not pass the "boiling test." This test is done by shaving a sliver of hide from a skin and boiling it to see if the tanning process is complete. A strip of skin properly chrome tanned will not curl up or harden if boiled in water. However, the best check for the complete tannage with these processes is the color of the skin. If a strip cut from the thickest part of the edge of the skin is all the same color, then the tanning solution has completely penetrated the skin.

Chrome tanning is a term used to indicate the tanning of a skin with chromium sulfate. This is an excellent chemical tan. Skins tanned with chrome will never lose their tannage even when soaked in water. It leaves the skin a light blue color and dye or vegetable-tanning substances are usually added to color the skin a natural shade. Alum-tanned and acid-tanned skins can be chrome tanned if desired and usually chrome tanning is preceded by acid tanning. Acids "open" the skin so the chrome salts will penetrate more completely. This is probably the best tannage to use for skins that will be made into garments. Chrome-tanned skins will pass the boiling test.

Vegetable tanning is tanning skins with tannin steeped from vegetable matter. Oak bark, hemlock bark, gambier, and terra japonica and a by-product of the wood pulp industry called Tannin-Blend are some of the products used for vegetable tanning. Vegetable tanning is probably the best tanning method used. Skins that are vegetable tanned are water resistant; they can be wetted, stretched, tooled, or made into almost any object that leather is used for with excellent results. The disadvantage is that vegetable tanning is very time consuming. In a commercial tannery, vegetable tanning is preceded by pickle tanning with acid. Skins tanned with vegetable matter will pass the boiling test.

Tanning chemicals are caustic and, in the case of sulfuric acid, burns can quickly result from the acid being spilled on bare skin. It will also quickly destroy clothing. All tanning chemicals are poisonous; therefore the home tanner should wear rubber gloves and goggles when working with these substances. They should also be kept safely away from children.

Degreasing the Skin

Some skins have to be degreased either before tanning, after tanning, or at both times. Degreasing is the act of removing an excess of oil and grease from the flesh or hair side of a skin because the excess grease might inhibit the tanning agents. Skins are also degreased after tanning if the hair is so full of oil it would soil everything it touches. Many skins must be degreased to remove the tanning oil before they are dyed. Beaver, bear, pig, and goat skins should always be degreased before they are tanned. In fact, it is a good rule to degrease any skin that you have doubts about.

Kerosene is a widely used degreasing agent. The skin is immersed in a kerosene bath and worked for a short time. Extremely greasy skins are soaked overnight in a kerosene bath to dissolve the grease. After a skin is degreased, the kerosene is washed out with a warm water and detergent bath. It also can be taken out by rubbing warmed sawdust into both the flesh and hair sides of the skin. Chlorinated hydrocarbons (dry cleaning fluids) are a fine degreaser, and they have the advantage of evaporating completely after the skin is removed from the bath.

Softening a Skin

After skins are removed from the tanning bath they are wet and pliable. As they dry they will shrink, shrivel, and get stiff if left unattended. To prevent this, the skin is stretched on a stretcher or drying frame and left until it has dried to the damp stage. Then it is taken off and staked or tumbled to soften the fibers.

If you have time to constantly attend the skin it can be "pulled" by hand as it dries to prevent it from shrinking. Pulling a skin means stretching it by grasping one section of skin and pulling it away from the other. The top should be pulled away from the bottom and the sides should be pulled away from each other so the skin is stretched in all directions. I pulled a deerskin very successfully by clamping a section in the vice and pulling on the opposite section with locking pliers. Both the vice jaws and the plier jaws were wrapped with tape to prevent skin damage.

If a skin shrinks excessively, it can be reshaped by dampening the skin and restretching it.

TOOLS FOR TANNING
Skinning Knives

Tanning processes are fairly uncomplicated, and very few special tools are needed to get started. The first tool needed will probably be a skinning knife to remove the hide from the animal, and almost any knife that can be sharpened can be used. The beginner will minimize accidental cuts in the skin by using a knife with a rounded point during the actual removal of the skin from the carcass. However, a pointed knife blade is helpful for making the initial opening cuts.

Wooden wedges are used to separate the skin from the carcass without cutting the tissues. Ropes, chains, or wire are needed for hanging the animal, and a tanning table will be used for some skinning jobs.

The Tanning Area

Tanning requires little space and entails little odor, so a basement or porch makes a fine area to work in, as long as the fleshing and dehairing is done outside. The home tanner could probably get along very well in a ten-foot-square space if no more space was available. Inside this area there should be a table, a fleshing beam, and some containers.

Containers for Tanning

Wooden or plastic containers are the best for home tanning since tanning chemicals will react with metals. A few plastic pails are needed for carrying liquids and for immersing small skins. If a wooden barrel is available, it is a good choice for a tanning barrel; but a large plastic garbage can with a locking lid will do just as well. A household scale is needed to weigh the skins and other ingredients, and a liquid measuring cup is convenient for measuring acids and other fluids. A wooden paddle is also needed for stirring liquids.

Fleshing Knives and Beams

Skins are fleshed by placing them hair side down over a hard surface and scraping the skin side with a knife. Fleshing knives are usually made in the shape of a knife blade, with a wooden handle at each end. One edge is sharpened like a knife or chisel and the back edge is left unsharpened. Special fleshing knives with teeth or with super sharp shaving blades are also used. The home tanner can get along at first by using a large tablespoon to flesh small skins and a large butcher knife to flesh large skins. Drive the point of the butcher knife into a block of wood to form a second handle.

A fleshing beam is usually shaped like a log and elevated at one end. However, it can be as simple as a section of the tanning table or a tree limb, or it can be as complicated as an adjustable fleshing beam made from fiberglass and metal. A very serviceable large beam can be made from a fence post and a small beam, from an eight foot section of one-by-eight-inch board.

Staking Boards

After skins are taken from the tanning solutions, they are softened by staking them. A staking board is a board sharpened to a V shape at one end. A section of skin is sawed back and forth over the edge (like shining shoes) to soften it. Some home tanners use a one-by-six-inch or wider board suspended edgewise between two supports. The section of skin is then sawed back and forth over the upright edge. Skins can also be suspended and beaten with a stick or placed in a large container with sawdust and walked on to soften them. Neat's-foot oil, cod-liver oil, or castor oil is swabbed on the skin during the softening process to aid in this procedure.

Water in the Tanning Process

Aside from the mentioned equipment, you will need a source of both soft water and tap water. Rainwater is about the best water for mixing in a tanning solution. Most well water contains minerals and other substances that can adversely affect the action of the tanning solutions or cause discoloring or streaking of the skins. In most climates, enough rainwater can be collected for a home-tanning operation by catching the water from the rain gutters on a house.

The next best source is well water that has been softened by being treated. If your home doesn't have it, you can probably obtain it from a neighbor at low cost. If neither is possible, there might be a lake, river, or stream nearby where the water is soft enough for tanning. The county extension agent or a local water-softening company can check it for softness.

Machinery in the Tanning Process

This about completes the articles needed for home tanning that are necessary. However, much of the process can be done by machinery if you get involved in a lot of tanning processes. A wringer-type washing machine does a fine job of rinsing, soaking, and wringing skins. It can do the job on a large skin with a fraction of the effort needed if you do all the work by hand. The back and forth action of the agitator will work the water through the skins, remove all dirt and foreign matter, and help to soften them. After they are rinsed, the skins can be run through the wringer at the top to squeeze out most of the water.

An automatic washer can be used for soaking and rinsing, and a clothes dryer with the heating element turned off makes an excellent tumbling drum for cleaning and softening hides.

After you gain experience in handling hides, you can save many steps or automate them to some extent. For instance, I have found that I can clamp my ¼-inch drill in the vise, put a rotary rasp in the chuck, and use the rotary rasp for fleshing small skins. This is done by holding a fold of skin over the forefinger and pushing it lightly against the rotating rasp. Care must be used not to push too hard, or the skin will be quickly ruined. However, if the operator experiments with a low value skin until he gets the feel of the operation, he can save time fleshing skins.

An electric drill can also be used for softening skins as a substitute for staking. First saw out a two-inch square section of hardwood and drill a ¼-inch hole in the center. Place a ¼-by-3-inch bolt in the hole, and turn a nut down against the wood so it won't slip; it may be necessary to glue the bolt in the wood also. Sand the hardwood block very smooth and then lubricate it with tanning oil or neat's-foot oil. Then fasten the block in the drill, clamp the drill in a vise, start the drill, and hold the skin against the rotating block. Ten minutes of this action can substitute for half an hour of hand staking.

Waiting for a skin to dry can consume a lot of valuable time, while a hair dryer will dry a skin very quickly.

There are several other items that are nice to have, even though you can probably get along without them. One is a skinning gambrel which holds an animal's hind legs apart when you are skinning them. It usually has a hook for hanging the animal up and two hooks for hooking under the hocks on each leg; and they come in a variety of sizes for animals from muskrats to cows.

Nearly everything a home tanner needs can be obtained from a tanner's supply outlet. This includes every type of skinning knife and fleshing blade, tail strippers for pulling the tailbone from small animal hides, nipper pliers for cutting off foot bones, special scrapers for removing tough membrane and flesh from hides, and a special breaking tool for softening skins that are laced into frames. Mechanical fleshers and drums are also offered for large numbers of hides. It is advisable to obtain the best tools you can afford.

Safety is a prime consideration in home tanning due to the many chemicals and substances used that are caustic or poisonous. The home tanner probably should wear rubber gloves and goggles at all times when handling chemicals.

OBTAINING TANNING SOLUTION MATERIALS

One of the most appealing aspects of home tanning is that most of the ingredients for making up the tanning solutions are commonly available from grocery stores and hardware stores. Sulfuric acid is widely used in industry and the most common source is auto parts stores where battery acid is available in most any amount that you need. This is 33⅓ percent sulfuric acid and the amount has to be increased when the tanning formula calls for pure sulfuric acid. Oxalic acid is also available from drug stores and some hardware stores.

Both ammonium alum and potash alum are available from drug stores, hardware stores, and farm supply outlets. Alum that is available from drug stores is more expensive because it must be pure; industrial alum is just as effective for tanning. The home tanner should also realize that the tanning substance in both types of alum is aluminum sulfate. In fact, when water is added to the alums, they become sulfuric acid and aluminum sulfate. Therefore, it is often more expedient for the home tanner to use aluminum sulfate instead of the alums for tanning. Aluminum sulfate is available from most any place where garden supplies are sold since it is used for treating garden soil.

The salt used for tanning is common sodium chloride that is non-iodized. Grocery stores and especially farm supply outlets carry untreated salt since it is used in animal feeds. Borax is carried by nearly all grocery stores as are washing soda (sodium carbonate), boric acid, and bicarbonate of soda.

Chromium potassium sulfate produces good leather, but it is a little hard to find. Usually it must be purchased from a chemical company or a tanning supply outlet, but since it does not deteriorate, large amounts can be purchased at one time and held for later use. The synthetic tanning substances are only available from tanning supply outlets and taxidermy supply houses.

Vegetable tanning supplies are literally all around us. Oak bark and hemlock bark are some of the tree barks that are highest in tannin. There is no need to shave the bark from a living tree to get a supply either. Sawmill yards where hardwoods are being converted into lumber usually have tons of it going to waste, but if you must take some from a living tree, just prune the tree and use the bark from limbs. Sumac and willow leaves also contain good amounts of tannin, and a favorite tanning substance for rabbit skins in early America was tea leaves. The frugal country folk saved the leaves after making tea until they had a quart or so; then they boiled them in just enough water to cover. This produced a dark tannin-rich liquid that they found would tan thin skins by simply immersing the skins in the solution and letting them soak until the tannin color penetrated the leather. A pinch of baking soda was often added to "sweeten" the mixture.

Dried alfalfa stems and leaves also are rich in tannin and have been found to produce a good tan. Alfalfa is, of course, used for hay, and the tannin from a bale of alfalfa would probably tan a dozen skins the size of a deer hide. A barkometer and pH indicator papers are very convenient to have if much vegetable tanning is anticipated.

Tannin is leached from bark and vegetable parts by immersing it in warm water. The main disadvantage of vegetable tanning is it is a rather tedious and time-consuming task. Simmering the plant parts for three hours is about the fastest way of extracting the tannin. However, if time isn't critical it is almost a foolproof way to tan skins.

2

Tanning Small Animal Skins: Beginning Projects

Tanning is an acquired skill, and probably no one is capable of doing top-notch work without considerable experience. Therefore, it is expedient to start with a small skin and gradually work into larger and more difficult projects. To begin we will skin, flesh, and tan a black squirrel skin.

TANNING FUR

Tanning Squirrel Fur

Black squirrels are rare and decorative enough to enhance anyone's den or game room. Interestingly enough, the northern part of the Lower Peninsula of Michigan is about the best place in the country to collect one. Turkey hunting near Alpena, Michigan last spring I saw over thirty squirrels and most were black. A Michigan Department of Natural Resources biologist confirmed that black squirrels, which are really the black phase of the grey squirrel, were by far the predominant color phase in that area.

Where I live in northern Wisconsin, black squirrels are very rare, but I finally spotted one when I was hunting grouse. It took nearly a week of returning to the same area before I again saw and collected the elusive tree dweller with a shotgun and #9 shot. This light shot minimized pelt damage so that it is impossible to find any holes in the tanned hide.

Skinning the Squirrel

Any animal is much easier to skin before the body heat has left and rigor mortis sets in because the hide is loose, the body is limp, and the skin slips off easily. After it has cooled, the hide seems to shrink to the animal, the tissues toughen, the leg and trunk will not flex easily, and skinning is several times harder.

Before skinning, brush the animal to remove burs, sticks, and mud that may have collected on the hair. The best time to remove the blood is before it dries by wiping with a damp cloth or by washing it off with cold water. If it dries, soften it by covering the bloody area with a damp cloth.

Hang the animal up by one hind leg using a string or piece of wire wrapped around the hock. Hang it about chest high which is a convenient height for skinning. Now sharpen a skinning knife to a keen edge and, starting at the foot pad on the free hind leg, make a cut along the back side of the leg, across the crotch in front of the anus, and up the back side of the other hind leg to a point where the wire is wrapped around the leg. Using the fingers and the knife very sparingly, work the skin loose from the free leg down to the body. Cut off the foot bones so you retain the claws on the leg skin. Then change the wire so the beast will hang from the skinned hind leg and skin the opposite leg. When both hind legs are skinned down to the tail, work the skin free around the base of the tail with your fingers. Using a tail puller or your fingers, remove the tailbone by holding the skin at the base of the tail and pulling the bone out of it, like pulling a finger out of a glove.

When the tailbone is out of the tail, carefully slit the tail from the base to the tip so the tail skin can lay flat. With the hind legs and tail skinned out, proceed to skin the rest of the animal by pulling downward on the skin. Very carefully cut around the anus and genitals, and continue working the skin towards the head, using the knife only when necessary. Carefully examine an area before using the knife and make sure you cut the tissue under the skin and not the skin itself. Take your time on the first skinning job and the next ones will be much easier.

Eventually you will encounter the front legs. Using the fingers, work the skin loose around the shoulders until you can pull the upper part of the leg far enough out of the skin to get your fingers around it. Then grasp the skin in one hand and the leg bone in the other and pull the leg out of the skin. It will "hang up" at the front pad and you will have to use the knife to skin out the foot leaving the claws on the skin.

Continue pulling the hide downward over the neck and head until the skin stops peeling at the base of the ears. Use the tip of the knife to cut off the ear cartilage at the base, then continue pulling the hide until it stops at the eyes. On a small animal, cut off the tissue at the eyes with just one cut, using only the tip of the knife. Pull the hide around to the mouth and nose and carefully cut away the tissue around these openings to free the hide.

After the hide is removed, it should be immersed in a weak solution of water and ammonia and then brushed again to remove all dirt and stains. Any solid matter on the skin can cause damage to the hide when it is fleshed.

The next step is to flesh the skin, removing all large bits of fat and meat. Use a fleshing knife or a large kitchen spoon that has been sharpened slightly with a file. For holding the hide, it is hard to beat the tapered fleshing beam used by trappers and fur buyers. Case-skinned hides like this one are slipped over the beam, and fleshing proceeds by pushing the fleshing knife from the head towards the tail. Remove all of the large pieces of flesh at this time; small or tightly attached pieces can be left on since they will loosen later when the hide is soaked. Be very careful not to gouge the skin or scrape it so close that the hair roots can be seen. When you finish the fleshing, weigh the hide and record the weight.

Salting the Hide

Now wash the hide in warm, soapy water, scrubbing it with a stiff brush to remove the blood or dirt wherever it is needed. Rinse it in clear, warm water to remove the soap and further clean it. Then partially dry the hide by swinging it around or wringing it out, and then put it back on the stretching board to damp dry. After the excess moisture is mostly gone, remove the hide from the stretching board and salt it. Use one pound (two cups) of salt for each pound of hide. Pour it on the flesh side of the skin and rub it in, making sure to get the edges and around the eyes, ears, and nose. Then roll it up, and place it on a board with one end slightly inclined so the moisture will drain out. Leave it this way for thirty-six hours. Then unroll it, scrape

off the old salt, resalt it again using one pound of salt to each pound
of hide, and roll it up again. This time leave it for forty-eight hours.
After forty-eight hours, hang it up by the nose and let it dry in a cool,
airy place away from the sun or artificial heat.

The hide is now salted and it is called a "green hide" or "green,
salted hide." It can be tanned immediately or held for up to six months
without tanning.

When a freezer is available, raw (unsalted) skins can be frozen
and held for up to one year. Turn the hide so the fur side is out, cover
the skin with newspaper, and roll it up so the newspaper forms a
package around the skin. Do not salt the skins before freezing them.

If you want to start tanning a hide immediately after skinning the
animal, soak the skin for eight hours in a saltwater solution made by
using one cup of salt to each gallon of warm water. Always use soft
water for tanning as hard water tends to stain the skin and hair.

Sometimes the best way to obtain a skin to tan is to buy it from
a fur buyer. Hides sold to commercial fur buyers are dried by the
trapper. If they have been well fleshed and carefully dried, they will
keep for up to a year. The first step in handling a dried skin is to soak
it as it will crack if folded or bent while dry. It will probably have to
be soaked overnight, but use clear, clean water for this process.

To get back to our squirrel skin, the next step is to soak the skin
in a borax solution. Use one ounce of borax to a gallon of warm water.
Weight the skin so it is completely covered by the solution and use a
paddle to agitate the skin occasionally. Be sure not to oversoak it as
the hair will loosen; approximately four hours should be enough. The
purpose of this soaking is to completely loosen all the tissues and meat
so the hide can be scraped clean.

Fleshing the Skin

After the soaking is complete, remove the hide from the solution,
wring it out by hand, and place it on the fleshing beam or a flat surface.
Use a fleshing knife or a spoon to scrape off all the remaining flesh and
meat. Be sure to remove the membrane that covers the hide: If this
tough, transparent membrane isn't removed, the tanning solution cannot penetrate the hide and it will dry stiff and hard. Do not press too
hard on the fleshing tool, especially with thin skins, as the hide will be
damaged. However, scrape every inch two or three times since it tends
to soften the skin by breaking up the fibers.

Tanning the Fur

Now the actual tanning can commence. This tanning method uses an oxalic acid solution. First obtain a plastic, glass, or wooden container that will hold a gallon of solution with plenty of reserve space. Don't use metal as it will cause a chemical reaction with the solution. Heat one quart of water to about 100° F. and dissolve one pint of salt and one ounce of oxalic acid crystals in it. Pour the solution into the tanning vat and add three more quarts of clear water to the mixture to produce a gallon of solution.

When the tanning solution has cooled, put the fleshed skin in it, and hold it down with a stone if that is necessary to make sure it is all covered by liquid. Agitate the skin several times and let it soak for about twenty-four hours. After twenty-four hours, remove the skin and rinse out the tanning solution as longer soaking could cause the hair to loosen.

It is important to halt the tanning process at this stage so it doesn't continue until the hide is "burned." Rinse the hide in a solution of one pound of borax in one gallon of water for ten minutes, stirring and working it to make sure the rinse penetrates every bit of the tanned hide. After ten minutes, take the hide out of the solution and rinse it in six changes of clean, cool water to remove all traces of the various solutions it has been subjected to.

Softening and Finishing

Wring the skin out and lay it flesh side up on a flat surface. Use the slicker to push all the water that you can get out of the skin, and then continue this process as long as you wish since it will help to soften it. Tack the skin on a stretcher and apply a coating of neat's-foot oil or castor oil. Leave the skin stretched until it is almost dry, then remove it from the stretcher and work the flesh side over a staking edge or the edge of a table until it is softened. If it dries before you are done, moisten it with a damp cloth and continue working it until it is soft. Softening is done by grasping one edge of the skin in each hand and sawing it back and forth as if you were shining shoes. Metal breaking rings also can be used for this but whatever you use, be sure the skin is pulled over a smooth surface so it doesn't become damaged.

After the skin is softened you can clean up the fur as the final step. Usually by this time the fur looks so matted and dull that you may wonder if it can ever be restored, but take heart. It will look very good when you finish cleaning and fluffing it. If it is very badly matted it should be washed in warm, soapy water and then rinsed in two or three changes of clear water. If a stain does not respond to this treatment, use naptha, benzine, or commercial dry cleaning fluid. Partially dry the skin and finish cleaning it by rubbing sawdust or cornmeal into the fur.

Start this cleaning method by warming up the sawdust or cornmeal in the oven or on top of the stove. If necessary, cool the material until you can handle it, but while it is still as warm as you can handle it, spread it over the fur and work it in to the roots. Rub all the material possible into the fur since every piece will pick up some dirt. When it is thoroughly rubbed in, let it set for thirty minutes so the dry material will absorb all liquid and free oil in the fur. If sawdust isn't available, oatmeal, chalk, or plaster of paris can be used.

To get the dry cleaning material out of the fur, shake it over newspaper or a large piece of cloth. It can be reused on the same fur if desired for a second cleaning. When the free material has been removed, comb the fur first in one direction and then the other to loosen the rest. If a vacuum cleaner is available you can use the cleaning attachment on that to remove the cleaning material from the fur.

The final step in tanning the squirrel skin is to lay it flesh side up on a flat surface. Use sandpaper or a damp cloth dipped in pumice stone to sand off any rough places on the hide. Any hard or stiff places can also be sanded so the skin will be pliable. Shake the skin very well to remove all loose sanding material, and apply a thin coat of castor oil to the flesh side of the fur. Be sure you don't use so much that it gets on the hair, and rub it in very well. This completes the tanning procedure for the black squirrel skin.

TANNING LEATHER

Tanning Raccoon Skin

For the second project, you can tan a small animal skin to use for leather. Surprisingly enough, some small animals have skin that is tough and thick enough to be used as shoelace and leather. Any beaver skins that have poor fur can be utilized for leather as can most furbearers and small domestic animals. An animal that is available in most any area of the country which will yield good leather is a raccoon, particularly an older animal. In areas where hunting isn't allowed, raccoons are often killed by cars or they can be trapped with steel or live traps.

Skinning the Raccoon

If possible, skin the raccoon immediately after it is killed since it will be much easier to get the hide off before the body heat leaves. Animals skinned for leather can be peeled in a different way than if they are to be tanned with the fur on. First wash the blood and dirt from the hide so the skinning knife won't cause more blood to be spread over the hair. Then lay the animal on its back on a bench at a convenient height, sharpen a good skinning knife, and make a cut that starts at the base of the tail and extends along the belly to the lower lips. Cut off the tail and set it aside to use for a wall decoration. Next cut up the inside of all four legs from the belly cut. Skin out the legs, being careful to get as little flesh and fat on the hide as possible; then work the skin off the belly on each side of the body, turning the carcass as you have to to remove the skin. Use the knife sparingly so you don't make any cuts through the hide.

Drying the Hide

The next step is to stretch the hide so it will dry without wrinkling and shrinking. For a raccoon skin a piece of plywood or even an old door will work for a stretching surface as long as it is portable. Lay the raccoon skin hair side down on the stretching surface, find a good handful of four-penny nails, and start by placing one nail at the nose. Be sure to drive the nails in securely enough so the shrinking hide won't pull them out. The next nail is driven at the base of the tail after the hide is pulled lengthwise enough to remove the slack from the skin. Then pull the sides of the skin to form a cross and nail them. Keep stretching and tacking the hide all around the perimeter to keep it fairly tight.

The skin should be left until it is cool and just starting to harden; this may take from only an hour or two in dry weather to four hours or longer. If you don't want to stretch the hide, it should be pulled in every direction about every half hour to keep it from shrinking and wrinkling. When it is cool, scrape the hide to remove all large pieces of flesh or fat. A large spoon works well for this; a fleshing knife will not be effective on this stretched hide. There is no need to knock yourself out at this stage to get all the excess fat and flesh off since the soaking and liming steps loosen stubborn deposits of excess material.

Salting the Skin

Now the hide must be salted. When this is done properly, the hide will keep up to six months if protected from insects and scavenger animals and kept cool. First remove it from the stretching board and weigh the hide to determine the amount of salt to use since it will take a pound of salt for each pound of hide. For a raccoon's skin, about eight cups of salt should be enough. Spread the hide out hair side down and cover the skin side with salt; be sure to get it right up to the edge of the skin and all around each part of the legs. Rub the salt in very well and make sure all the tissue is treated. This is actually the first step of the chemical action of the tanning process, and it should be done with care.

When the salt has been evenly applied, fold the skin in half salted side in and roll it up tightly. Next, place it on a board that has one end raised so it is inclined. After two days, unroll the hide, shake away any loose salt, and resalt the hide again using a pound of salt to each pound of hide. Rub this second application in very well as before, and roll it up, setting it on an inclined surface so it will drain. After two more days, unroll the hide and let the skin dry hair side down, away from artificial heat and out of the sun. The hide may be stored this way, or it can be soaked and the rest of the tanning can proceed immediately.

When you are ready to start the tanning procedure, scrape off the loose salt and fill a plastic pail full of warm rainwater or other soft water. Add one ounce of borax for every gallon of water, and put the hide in the borax solution to soak for three to five days, stirring it three or four times a day. This step is done to loosen the flesh and fat and the membrane that covers the hide, but don't worry if it also loosens the hair since it will be removed anyway. When the flesh is loosened, remove the skin from the solution and rinse it in clear water, squeezing and wringing the hide to remove the borax solution.

Fleshing the Hide

The next step is one of the most important of the tanning steps since it involves scraping away all of the remaining flesh and fat and particularly the membrane that covers the skin. This membrane is almost impervious to water and unless it is removed the hide will take the tanning solution unevenly and it will pucker when dried.

No fat or flesh should be left on the skin when you finish this step and the skin should be white, soft, and pliable. It is easy to miss the flesh at the edge of the skin so care must be used to be sure this hard-to-see material is also scraped away. When you finish, the skin should be white and smooth and soft, with the derma layer exposed. However, be careful not to overdo the fleshing process to the point where the skin is scraped away and the hair roots are visible since this will weaken the leather.

Dehairing the Skin

The next step is to remove the hair. This is done by soaking the hide in a dehairing solution of water and lime or water and lye. I have successfully loosened the hair from small animal skins and deer hides by adding a good shovelful of wood ashes to each gallon of water in the dehairing solution. This is a bit messy and imprecise so the beginner might want to stick to one of several established dehairing formulas such as lime water.

First find a wooden or plastic pail that will hold at least four gallons of water. Measure enough soft water or rainwater into the pail to completely cover the raccoon skin (approximately three gallons). Next add ½ pound of agricultural lime and stir the solution until the lime is dissolved in the water. Then put the skin in the solution and let it soak, stirring it once or twice a day, until the hair comes off easily. The hair will probably be loosened in about three days, but it can take up to two weeks depending upon the weather. The hide has to be kept completely submerged, so place a rock on it if it tends to float. I use a rubber glove on one hand to pull on the hair to see if it is loose enough. It should come off very easily when you pull on it; if tension is felt, it should be soaked for a day or two more.

When the hair is properly loosened, remove the hide from the solution and hang it up for a few minutes to drain; then put it across your fleshing beam, fur side up. The knife-edge of the fleshing knife can be used for dehairing if you are experienced with its use. If not, use the back side to scrape the hair away, using the same long smooth motions that are commonly used for removing the flesh from skins. The hair is set in a porous layer of skin and this should be scraped away so that the skin is white. Removing the hair is a comparatively easy, swift process, and a skin can be dehaired in a short time.

When the hair and hair roots have all been removed and the hide is clean and uniform, the deliming process can proceed. Rinse the hide very well in six changes of water; and then put it in a clean container, cover it with clean water, and let it soak overnight. The next morning, dump the water and recover the skin with fresh water as before, but add ½ pint of vinegar to each five gallons of water. Soak the hide in this solution for twenty-four hours, stirring it at least three times during this bath. Then empty the vinegar solution, refill the pail with fresh water, and again let it soak overnight. After this the tanning solution can be applied to the skin.

Tanning the Hide

Although many tanning solutions are available commercially, for the first tanning job, I suggest bark tanning the skin. Bark-tanned leather is tough, traditionally colored, and as water resistant and durable as leather can be. However, the solution takes time to produce and the home tanner should make it up well before the hide is dehaired and made ready to tan.

The first step is to find some tree bark. All oak bark can be used as can sumac, butternut, maple, or hemlock. Peel off about nine pounds of the outer bark, and chop it up with a hatchet until the pieces are small enough to fit into a grinder. I use a hand gristmill. Grind the bark up as fine as possible, and then add two gallons of hot water to three pounds of the ground bark which has been placed in a five-gallon wood, stone, or plastic container. This will have to soak about fourteen days. If a clear container can be found, such as a large glass jar, the solution can be set out in the sun where it will be kept warm. This will cause it to work much faster and the solution can be ready to use in one week. Even if the pail can be kept warm (up to 90° F.) by being placed near continuous artificial heat, the tannin will leach out into the water much faster, and a stronger solution will result.

Start the tanning process by placing the skin in a plastic pail, covering the top with a cloth, and pouring the bark solution through it so the bark bits will be strained out. If some water has evaporated, add enough soft water to bring it up to the original two gallons. Add one-half cup of vinegar, and soak the hide in this solution for two weeks. It should be stirred at least twice a day and its position changed so it will be colored evenly.

As soon as you have the hide soaking in the bark solution, pour two gallons of hot water over another three pounds of bark and start it soaking. Continue to stir the skin in the tanning solution and watch it closely. When an examination reveals that the surface of the hide has taken an even color (after about fourteen days), it is time to proceed to step two of the leather tanning method.

Take one quart of the tanning solution out, and add one quart of the new solution that has steeped for two weeks and another one-half cup of vinegar. Every five days, take out an additional gallon and add a gallon of the new solution until the new solution is all used up. Let the hide soak in this new solution for an additional fifteen days; then remove the hide and add the remaining three pounds of bark directly to the solution already in use. Stir it up well and then put the hide back in the solution, making sure it is completely covered. Leave the hide in the solution until the test for tanning shows it is done, which may take about four weeks.

The test for tanning is used for every bark tanned hide and it simply means that you slice off a thin sliver of hide from the edge of the skin and examine it. If it looks like it's colored evenly all the way through, drop the piece in a pan of water and boil it for about five minutes. A piece of hide that is incompletely tanned will curl up and harden. Boiling will not affect a well-tanned hide. If the test shows a skin to be incompletely tanned, return it to the solution and let it soak another two weeks and then retest.

Softening and Finishing the Leather

When the skin is completely tanned, remove it from the solution, wring it out, and nail the hide to a flat surface after it is pulled taut. After it has dried somewhat, lay it skin side down and wipe the outer surface with a coating of warm neat's-foot oil. Let it continue drying, removing it from the stretching board while still damp.

To soften the hide, work the skin back and forth across a staking board or other smooth hard surface in a seesaw fashion. This was previously explained under tanning furs, but in this case the leather is turned over and each side is worked.

Every inch should be rubbed, and if the hide dries it should be moistened and the staking process resumed. Keep it up as long as you have the patience because the longer you do this the softer the leather will become. When you are satisfied it is as soft as it will become, dampen it again and then apply a coat of dubbin leather preserver.

Dubbin can be purchased, but it also can be made by melting beef tallow and combining it with equal amounts of castor oil: about ⅓ pound of each will more than treat the raccoon skin. Apply the dubbin to the hide by rubbing it in very well, staking it again, and then rubbing in more dubbin. About three applications should combine the dubbin and skin very well.

To finish the leather, sandpaper off any rough places on the surface of the skin and give it a final coating of dubbin.

3

Tanning Small Furbearers

All of the skins covered in this chapter are tanned with the fur on, and they are relatively thin. Therefore, each can be tanned with every formula listed, even though the formula might be described under another animal. The most economical and uncomplicated procedure is the aluminum sulfate and salt formula recommended for muskrat skin tanning. The most complicated procedure, chrome tanning, is described under skunk skin tanning and produces the most permanent and versatile leather.

Skins can be tanned with aluminum sulfate and kept until the necessary amounts are accumulated for a project; then, if desired, they can be retanned with chrome. All of the materials used for tanning are caustic or poisonous, so wear gloves and eye protection whenever they are handled. Keep out of reach of children. If taken internally, administer egg white and consult a doctor immediately.

TANNING MUSKRAT FUR

The first fur skin covered is the muskrat. The muskrat has been called the backbone of the fur industry with good cause. They are very prolific, extremely easy to trap, and they yield a fine soft fur that closely resembles mink fur.

Trapping Muskrat

Like many other boys that raised in a rural environment, I depended on trapping muskrat in the fall as a source of spending and school clothes money. Moreover, I have depended on muskrat trapping several times in my life to supplement my income even after I was grown and had a family. I will pass along some hints on trapping for the "marsh rat" for readers who might want to make some pocket money or trap enough 'rats and tan them so they can be made into a coat or other fur garment.

Muskrats can usually be caught where they have made feed beds, dug holes in the bank, or built houses. Feed beds are circular patches of dug up grass roots or cattail stems that are floating on the surface. The muskrat uses one of these floating beds for a raft to keep his head above water while he is eating. The trap is set right in the center of the feed bed, and when the muskrat comes to dine he will usually get caught. Den holes in the bank are very attractive to muskrats, and they seem to visit each one at least once every night, and many times they live in them. Muskrat houses can be noticed as dome-shaped piles of vegetation that the muskrats have entered from the bottom and hollowed out for sleeping and eating space. Around the perimeter of the house there is usually a ledge that the muskrats use to rest on while they are making frequent repairs to their house and the trap is set on this ledge.

The greatest source of disappointment in muskrat trapping is the way they will "wring" out of a trap if it is not set correctly. Wring outs are almost completely eliminated by using stop loss–type traps and setting them so the muskrat can reach deep water and drown.

Skinning the Muskrat

Muskrats are about the easiest animals to skin, in fact, some champion-type skinners can strip the hide from a muskrat in fifteen seconds. While attending college, my son skinned muskrats for a commercial fur buyer who paid fifteen cents a muskrat. My son could make ten to fifteen dollars a day after school, using a method that is standard for professional skinners.

Standing at a bench, grasp the muskrat by the right hind leg and straighten it out so the weight is hanging from the leg. This pulls the skin tight so you can insert the point of the knife under the heel just

A muskrat and a skinning knife. Muskrat fur is soft and fine and can be made into fine garments. If you tan your own, you can save a considerable amount on the cost of a coat.

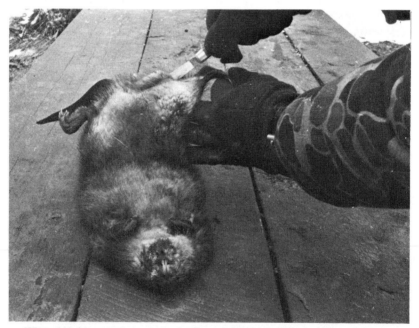

When skinning a muskrat, make the first cut across the hind legs from heel to heel.

above the black skin of the foot. Using a sharp knife with a skinning tip, cut along the back of the legs to the crotch. Now go to the other hind leg and do the same so the cuts join. Use your fingers to work the hide loose from the belly up to the rib cage. Work the skin loose from the legs with your fingers, and if you use force you can pull the skin loose from the heel and there is no need to cut it. Also work the skin loose behind the tail on the back and try to pull it loose from the tail area.

When the skin is all loose around the hind legs, belly, and back, grasp the hind legs in one hand and the belly skin in the other, and pull in opposite directions to peel the skin off like a glove towards the head. When you get to the front legs, grasp the leg skin in one hand and the leg in the other, turning the leg skin inside out, and pull hard enough to separate the two without using a knife.

After the front legs are free, continue pulling on the skin until you get to the head. When the ears become visible as two small white bits of skin, cut them off at the base and then pull the skin to the eyes and carefully cut around them. Strip the skin to the nose and mouth, cut off the nose, and leave it on the skin. Be extremely careful with the head and you will wind up with a good-looking pelt.

Fleshing the Skin

Special wire stretchers are made for stretching muskrat pelts. The pelt is turned so the flesh side is out; then the hide is slipped over the

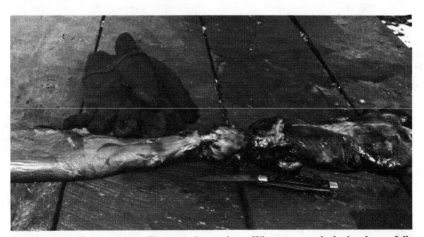

Pull the skin off the muskrat like removing a glove. When you reach the head, carefully cut around the eyes and ears. The nose and lips are carefully trimmed loose from the carcass and left on the skin.

stretcher, pulled tight, and fastened to hooks on the bottom of the stretcher. The pelt is left on the stretcher until it is dried, which doesn't take very long: In dry weather, a muskrat hide will dry in two to three days.

Before they are put on the stretcher, muskrat hides are usually fleshed on a beam with a small fleshing knife. Because muskrat hides are thin, the fleshing knife must be used carefully when removing the inner membrane as well as all flesh and fat. If the hide can't be fleshed properly the way it is, soak it for about two hours in a borax solution made by dissolving one ounce of borax in a gallon of soft water. Flesh it again after the borax has softened the flesh and fat; rinse the skin well, and you are ready to start tanning.

Tanning the Fur

Aluminum sulfate and common salt are economical and easily obtained substances that will produce a fine tan for fur skins. This type of tan leaves the hair its natural color and bleaches the skins to a soft white while shrinking them to "set" the hair permanently in place. Only if the skins are going to be in contact with water would this tan be unsatisfactory, and in this case the skins can be retanned with chrome or vegetable tan.

Prepare the salt-alum mixture by mixing four ounces of salt and four ounces of aluminum sulfate together in five pints of hot water. Stir until the solids are dissolved, allow the mixture to cool, and immerse the properly fleshed skins in the mixture for forty-eight to seventy-two hours or until the skin has turned white clear through. Be sure and leave the skin long enough since longer immersion will do it no harm.

Muskrat skins can also be well tanned with a tawing paste made of aluminum sulfate, potash alum, or ammonium alum. Prepare the salt-alum mixture by mixing ½ pound ammonia or potash alum, one ounce of washing soda, and four ounces of salt. Dissolve the ingredients in a minimum of water and then add wheat flour to make a paste. Spread a thick layer of paste on the flesh side of the skin, cover it to keep it from drying out, and let it set for three days before scraping off the old paste and applying a new covering. Do this twice and then test the skin for tanning. If it isn't done, repeat the layer and allow to set for three more days. This method tends to shrink the skin and hold the fur in place better than some other methods which swell the hide.

Now completely immerse the hide in a borax solution for ten

Pull the skin over a fleshing beam and use a butcher knife or fleshing knife to remove all the meat, fat, and membrane from the skin. Use great care as muskrat skins are very thin.

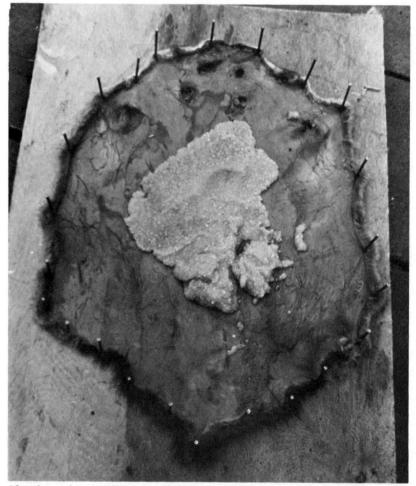

After the muskrat is skinned, carefully slit the skin down the center of the belly and tack it on a stretching frame to "taw" tan it.

minutes, alternately wringing it out and returning it to the water. Rinse the fur in several changes of fresh, clean water to remove the borax.

Squeeze the water out of the skin with your hands, and lay it out fur side down on a flat surface. Push as much water as you can out of the skin with a slicker. Finally, tack it down to a wooden surface, stretching it taut before you nail it. Apply a good coating of neat's-foot oil and just before it is completely dry, take it off the stretcher and start vigorously softening it over a staking board. If it dries completely, dampen it by wrapping it in a damp cloth for an hour, and then resume the staking action. The skin should be staked until it is as soft as cloth.

TANNING WEASEL FUR

The next project, a weasel, is tanned using the oxalic acid tanning method. There are several different varieties of weasels in North America, but the largest is the long-tailed weasel which might grow to eighteen inches from nose to tail. This is the weasel that the home tanner would probably want to trap for making into a wall decoration or an article of clothing since its winter coat is a beautiful white.

Trapping Weasel

The best way to locate a weasel is to look for his tracks in the snow. They jump with two feet together and their track looks like a print made by holding the fingers together and pushing just the tips of the fingers into the snow. If you follow the track for some distance, it will probably disappear into a clump of grass or under the roots of a small tree: This is the place to set a trap.

Find a snow-covered clump of grass and kick an opening in the snow and grass down to the ground. You will have created a hole or cave in which to set the trap. Be sure the back of the opening is blocked off by a tree or a hump in the ground, but in the front the snow should be cleared away in a path for the weasel to enter. If rabbits or grouse

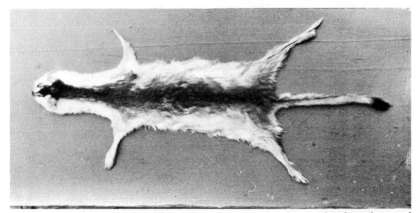

This weasel skin has a very appealing two-toned color because it was taken from the weasel in the fall when it was in the midst of turning from a brown summer coat to a white winter coat.

are being hunted, the entrails and feathers or fur make very good bait. Put the entrails and the head of the prey in the back of the cubby or trap site and make a nest for the trap out of the feathers or rabbit fur at the entrance of the cubby. Set the trap in the nest, cover it with fur, and arrange the grass so it forms a roof over the trap so no snow can fall on it. Finally, scatter a few feathers or some rabbit fur around outside the cubby so the weasel will be sure to investigate when he comes by.

Weasels move at intervals of about a week so don't worry if you don't catch him for awhile. A good trap for the weasel is the #1 or #1½. Be sure to partially depress the pan so it will spring easily; weasels are very light steppers and won't spring the trap otherwise. If tracks in the snow show where the weasel had come by without entering your cubby, put fresh bait on it and scatter a good supply of feathers around again.

The weasel will probably be instantly killed by the trap and he will be frozen stiff when you check. Pick up the trap, take it home, and thaw it out before removing the animal from inside. If you don't do this the steel of the trap will probably rip the thin skin of the weasel when you remove him.

Skinning and Fleshing the Weasel

Skin the weasel as soon as he is thawed. Although weasels are case skinned in the same way as squirrels or mink, they are usually very lean and the hide is more difficult to pull off. Because the hide is also thin, extra care should be used to avoid ripping it when it is removed. Before you start skinning, wash all blood and dirt from the pelt. If he gets a little damp, hang him up for awhile until he dries. Fleshing the pelt can usually be done in just a few minutes with a sharp knife by pinching the flesh and fat between your thumb and the knife blade.

Weasel fur can also be salted before it is tanned to open up the pores of the hide and allow the tanning solution to penetrate better. If you wish to tan the hide immediately, dissolve ½ cup of salt in two quarts of warm, soft water. Immerse the hide in the solution, making sure it is entirely covered, and let it soak for six hours.

When you remove the weasel fur from the solution, flesh it again, and this time be sure to remove all the flesh and fat and to break down the thin membrane that covers the skin. If the membrane doesn't come off easily, scrape it with an instrument with teeth like a table fork or a steak knife.

Tanning the Hide

When this is done, mix up an oxalic acid solution of one gallon of warm soft water with two cups of salt and two ounces of oxalic acid. *Caution:* This is a poisonous solution; don't inhale the fumes or allow anyone to drink it. Be sure to dispose of it properly so it doesn't contaminate water supplies.

Immerse the weasel skin in the solution, letting it soak for twenty-four to forty-eight hours and stirring it often. When it is tanned, wash the solution out by immersing the skin in a borax solution as described in chapter 2 on tanning a squirrel skin.

TANNING SKUNK FUR

The third skin we will tan is a skunk skin. Skunks have beautiful fur and tough skin, and they are a fine product when properly tanned. Everyone knows that a skunk smells bad and it is this prejudice that keeps it from being used more often than it is. In the days before the proper name had to be used for furs, skunk coats were a fast seller under the name of alaskan sable or black sable.

Trapping Skunk

Due to the low prices paid for skunk fur and their natural defense system, this animal is over abundant in most areas. Therefore, any interest in utilizing this animal is not only beneficial to the skunk family, but to all wildlife and even mankind since they are a prime carrier of rabies.

Skunks frequent garbage dumps, old farmsteads, the edges of large fields, and most other places where woods and fields are intermingled. They are not naturally wary and are therefore easily trapped. If they are caught in a leg hold trap and then shot, they spray scent all over and the job of skinning and tanning the hide is a miserable one.

Fortunately, there are ways to trap the skunk so it doesn't smell. They don't usually release scent when they are caught in a live trap and dropped in water and drowned. If you don't care to take a chance, a #220 Conibear-type trap will immediately kill the skunk when he trips it. This type of trap looks like an open-ended box when it is set, and when the animal springs it it clamps the beast around the body or head. For reasons known only to the skunk, when the trap springs and the animal is killed it almost never sprays, and all the trapper needs to do is take it out of the trap and skin it. If the trap is checked often it is likely the animal can be found before it stiffens up and this will make skinning much easier.

Skinning the Skunk

Skinning a skunk is a precarious venture for the uninitiated because the scent can still be released in large amounts if undue pressure is applied to the scent glands or if they are cut. However, many men have skinned hundreds of skunks with hardly a mishap. Be sure to wear rubber gloves and old clothes, and use a very sharp knife so it doesn't pull the skin when you are making the cuts around the rear end.

Skunks are case skinned, so start by hanging the animal about chest high by one hind leg. Use wire instead of rope for hanging it so you don't accidentally cut it loose when you are skinning. The sharp jolt of the skunk hitting the ground might squirt the scent out. Cut the skin loose all around both hind paws by circling the hocks with the knife, then make a cut up the inside of the hind legs to the vicinity of the anus. This is the problem area since the scent bags, which look like puffed up areas, are located on each side of the anus. When you reach this area, make the knife cuts carefully around them so they are not disturbed. Continue the knife cut to the tail, skin out the base of the tail, and pull the bone out of the skin, slitting the tail so it lays open. Pull the skin down over the body to the front legs. If the skin sticks to the carcass, carefully use the tip of the knife to cut it loose since pulling could squeeze the scent out of the glands.

When you reach the front legs, pull the leg up through the skin to the hock area and cut the skin loose by circling the top of the paw with the knife. Continue pulling the skin down over the head and use the knife to cut off the base of ears and eyes. Also cut the lip and nose areas to free the skin, taking care not to nick your hands with the teeth of the skunk.

Fleshing the Skin

Although most skunks are fat and a lot of the flesh is going to come off with the skin, they are very easy animals to flesh. Pay attention to the tail, eyes, and nose, laying them flat and scraping away any remaining flesh and fat. As always, take care not to scrape the hide so close that the hair roots show.

Degreasing the Skin

Skunk skins must be degreased to remove excess grease and odor from the skin. Immerse the skin in kerosene, white gasoline, or a commercial dry cleaning fluid and wash it for at least twenty minutes, plunging and working it by hand. Then remove it and wash the skin in a detergent solution made by mixing two tablespoons of Ivory or Tide detergent to each gallon of water. A more economical way to degrease the skunk hide is to pour about one pint of kerosene in a gallon of coarse sawdust and to rub the mixture into both the fur and flesh sides of the hide. After letting the skin stand for two hours, hang it up by the snout and beat the sawdust completely out of it with a switch or paddle. Now rinse the skin in several changes of water to remove any remaining sawdust and dirt, and the actual tanning process can begin.

Tanning the Hide

Most likely, the skunk skin will be made into a wall hanging or an article of clothing. For a wall hanging the skin can be alum tanned, but if it is to be used for a garment, the chrome tan process would be better.

Skunk pelts stretched for drying. Skunk pelts are easy to get, easy to tan, and have a ready market for wall hangings, especially when they are scented with an appealing perfume.

After the skin is degreased and rinsed, wait until the hair is dry and the flesh side of the skin is just damp. The mix one pound of salt in one gallon of water and immerse the skunk skin in this solution for half an hour. While the skin is soaking, mix six ounces of chrome crystals in two quarts of hot tap water. After the skunk skin has soaked in the saltwater for half an hour, remove it and pour half of the chrome solution in the container, stirring it well. Reimmerse the skunk skin in this mixture for ten to twelve hours, stirring it every four hours. Remove the skin, add the rest of the solution, and this time let the skin soak until it is tanned clear through—about forty-eight hours. Be sure to leave the skin long enough so the blue chrome color has soaked completely through.

Softening and Finishing Skunk Fur

When the tanning is complete, remove the skin and rinse it in several changes of clear water. Squeeze out the excess water, and then neutralize and oil the skin by swabbing an ammonia oil mixture on the skin.

To make an ammonia oil mixture, mix one cup of neat's-foot oil, one cup of warm water, and two ounces of household ammonia together. Swab this on the flesh side of the skin in three successive coats, allowing each to soak in before adding another. Turn the skin hair side out while the coats of oil are soaking in. Keep the hair as dry as possible with a fan or hair dryer. After the third coat of oil, let the skin set overnight, then stake it until it is soft. If the skin won't soften sufficiently after this treatment, brush the flesh side with an oil mixture made by combining eight ounces of sulfonated neat's-foot oil and one pint of water. After the flesh side is well coated with this oil, hang the skin up to dry completely.

In a day or two after it has dried completely, lay the skunk skin flat and use a sponge to dampen the flesh side of the skin with a carbolic acid solution made by adding one half ounce of carbolic acid to one gallon of water. Make sure all of the skin is damp, roll it up, put it in a plastic bag, and tie the top of the bag.

Leave it overnight, and the next day the skin should be soft enough to be staked by stretching it over a fleshing beam and scraping it with a fleshing knife. If it doesn't need any further fleshing, use the back of the knife to stretch and make the skin pliable or work it over a staking board so the fibers will be stretched. If the skin seems excessively dry, brush on some of the oil mixture while you are working the skin.

When it seems as pliable as it is going to get, heat up a gallon of sawdust and work it into both the hair and flesh sides. Leave it for a few minutes so it will absorb the oil, and then hang the skin and beat it with a paddle or switch until the sawdust is removed.

Any thick or hard places in the skin should be shaved with a knife or sanded with fine sandpaper until they are thin enough to be pliable. Be careful not to make the skin so thin that the hair roots show through.

TANNING MINK FUR

Almost any home tanner is going to want to try tanning a mink skin after he gains some experience. The mink is probably the most well known of all the furbearers, and many a lady has been thrilled by the luxurious sensation of having a mink draped over her shoulders. Mink coats are usually very expensive, costing as much as a good automobile at least. But let's take a look at this animal and examine his habits so we will know more about how he lives and how to catch one (or even several) for a home tanning project.

The wild mink is brown or dark brown and about two feet long. The males are much larger than the females; many females are only about eighteen inches long. The males might weigh nearly four pounds, while adult females might only weigh about one and one half pounds. Male mink are much more valuable to the fur trade and usually sell for twice as much as the females.

Mink live near water, but they are not strictly a water animal as the muskrat and beaver are, and especially during the summer they may not enter the water for weeks at a time. However, they get a large percentage of their food from the creeks and ponds in their territory.

Mink feed on most every small mammal, fish, or bird, but it is interesting to realize that in summer the crayfish is the dominant food while in winter, rabbits, muskrats, and mice make up most of their diet. Wild mink that are well fed will stay along the same half-mile section of creek bank but when they get hungry they will travel for twenty miles or more to find a good food supply. Moreover, they may travel overland crossing fields, mountains, and even going through large cities looking for a new home.

Trapping Mink

Mink are not exceedingly hard to trap by a trapper versed in their habits, particularly since they are only partially shy of man's scent or disturbances to their trails. Probably the most effective trap is a pocket set that is made along a well-traveled runway.

Mink are creatures of habit, and if you follow a stream for a ways you will sooner or later see where a high bank, tree roots, or even a large rock will guide the mink into entering the water as he makes his weekly runs up and down the creek. If this water is less than a foot deep, it will probably be a good place to make the set. Find a place where the bank is fairly vertical with a water depth of one foot or less, and take a trapper's trowel or small tiling spade and dig a round, half-submerged hole horizontally into the bank, right at the waterline. Dig back in the bank about eighteen inches and slant it upward another six inches so the back of the hole is well above the waterline.

A hole in the bank is a natural attraction to mink, and when a new hole appears along his travel route, the mink is sure to investigate it. He will probably do this the first time he comes by unless he is distracted at the time by other prey or danger. However, trappers make it even more attractive with bait and scent.

To bait the set, take the skinned rib cage with the lungs, heart, and liver intact from a muskrat carcass and rub it around on the bank in the vicinity of the hole, and then push it up into the hole so it rests in the topmost part which is above the waterline. This tempting morsel will send out strong food odors to a mink that investigates the new excavation. Pull a good handful of soft marsh grass or dry moss, put one or two drops of good mink scent on the soft material and push it up into the hole so it rests against the bait. This will signal to a mink that a fresh kill has been made and that another mink has tried to hide it. The mink will probably lose all his natural caution as he tries to steal the food that he thinks another mink has left.

At the entrance to the hole, place a #1½ trap that has been dyed or painted black to look like the creek bottom. Partially depress the pan so it springs easily and bed the trap right at the entrance so any mink that tries to enter will spring it. Then stake the trap out in deep water so when the mink gets caught he will drag the trap out and quickly drown.

Check your traps at least once a week and when you catch the mink, take him home and dry his fur out as soon as possible. If he is dirty, wash him thoroughly, and once the fur is dried, start skinning the mink. A hair dryer works very well for drying, just don't put the fur so close to heat that it will burn your hand, because it will damage the skin also.

Skinning the Mink

Hang the mink up by one hind leg about chest high and make a knife slit through the footpad and up the inside of the hind leg to the anus. Circle the anus and continue up the inside of the other hind leg till you get to the wire or clamp that is holding the opposite foot.

Now use the fingers to pull the skin off the leg and footpad. Use the tip of the knife to cut toes off from the inside so the claws are retained on the skin. Skin out the base of the tail, pull the tailbone out, and slit the tail skin up the center. Now change the wire over to the other foot and finish skinning out the left foot. Continue pulling the skin down over the mink's body by grasping the body in one hand and the skin in the other. You shouldn't have to use the knife again until you get to the front feet which are also cut off from the inside, leaving the claws and toes on the skin. Mink fur is very valuable and great care should be used in skinning. Make the customary cuts around the ears, eyes, nose, and lips.

Fleshing the Skin

Mink usually have a minimum of fat on their skins, but any meat and membrane must be broken up and removed before the tanning can commence. In most commercial mink ranches, the fleshing is done immediately after the animal is skinned, but I have had the best luck fleshing a mink after it has been placed on the fleshing board and allowed to partially dry. Then I very carefully peel away the excess flesh and membrane using a sharp knife, and I rinse the hide in clear water to remove all dirt and bits of tissue from the skin or hair.

Tanning the Hide

The oxalic acid solution or chrome tanning will be satisfactory for tanning the mink skin, but if the hair tends to be loose or if the mink skin will be used to line some article of clothing where it will receive alot of wear, the alum tanning should be used.

The salt-acid solution of "pickle" tanning will also give satisfactory results for tanning the mink skin. Probably the main advantage is its ease and the casual way it can be handled, especially if you can't give the hide close attention. Actually this solution can be used two different ways: It can be painted on the flesh side of the hide, or the entire hide can be immersed in the liquid.

After the skin is softened, slit it up the center of the belly, being very careful to keep the cut on the center line. Lay the skin out on a thick layer of newspaper and proceed to mix up a thick tanning paste made by mixing one half ounce of pure sulfuric acid or two ounces of battery fluid into one pound of salt. Add just enough water to make a thick paste of the salt solution and then spread it on the skin; put it only on the flesh side, but be sure to cover it very well. When the skin is thoroughly covered, lay a sheet of plastic over it and leave it for six hours or until it dries. The object is to keep the paste from drying out before it has a chance to penetrate the skin.

After six hours, scrape off the paste with a knife and apply a fresh coat. Leave the second coat covered for four hours and then check the skin for proper tanning according to the tanning test. If it looks good, leave the tanning solution uncovered until it dries and then scrape off and rinse out the pickle solution by immersing the skin in a neutralizing solution. Make the antacid solution by adding ½ cup of sal soda or one pint of vinegar to a gallon of water. Leave the skin in the solution overnight, and the next morning rinse it in several changes of water and proceed to soften it.

The mink skin can also be tanned in a liquid pickle solution made by combining one gallon of soft water, four ounces of battery-type sulfuric acid, and one quart of salt. Mix this solution very well and immerse the skin in it. Let it soak for three days, remove it, and then neutralize the skin by soaking it in one gallon of water which has a pint of vinegar stirred into it.

Finishing the Mink Fur

A skin tanned with the sulfuric acid method will be softer than with some other methods but it still must be staked and drummed to make it an attractive fur. A wooden staking board works very well for staking the mink skin. Keep adding tanning oil and keep working it across the staking board until it is as soft as cloth. If the fur needs degreasing when you finish, mix a good handful of warmed sawdust into the fur and then shake it out.

TANNING RABBIT FUR

When it comes to tanning fur skins, it is well to practice on a cheap skin before you commit a good mink or other valuable fur to a process that you aren't familiar with. A skin that is available to most anyone and easy to acquire is a wild or domestic rabbit skin. Although there are many varieties, three types are most common: the cottontail, the snowshoe hare, and the jackrabbit. The jackrabbit has the thickest skin and the snowshoe has the most appealing and warmest fur. However, any rabbit skin is warm and the rabbit hides you tan can be used as liners in gloves or mittens which will protect against most any kind of cold.

The snowshoe or varying hare is found in the north. It is brown in the summer and turns a beautiful white when winter comes. They have population cycles and vary from 600 to the square mile in a good year to less than 50 in a very poor year. Canadian Indians make blankets and line outer garments with the varying hare skins. They are very warm but tend to shed their hair on a continuing basis and therefore are unsuitable for wear by most people. When the hide is tanned, cut into strips, sewn into a blanket, and the blanket sewn between cloth, it doesn't shed.

Skinning the Rabbit

Start tanning the rabbit by either case skinning or flat skinning it. The case-skinning methods have been described under mink tanning; but to flat skin a rabbit, lay him on his back and cut off the head and all four feet. Then make a slit up the belly from the crotch to the neck. Use the fingers to work the skin off the belly to the legs. Then make slits up the inside of each leg from the belly to the point where the leg was cut off. Use your fingers to work the skin off the legs and peel back the skin around the neck, down the back, and pull it off the rear end. A rabbit skin is thin, and usually very little, if any, fat comes off with it; but scrape it with a butcher knife or fleshing knife anyway to stretch the fibers. The inner membrane will probably not come off.

Tanning the Hide

Many rabbit raisers use the sulfuric acid or alum tanning formulas. Each of these formulas will tan three skins. The salt-alum mixture is made by combining one-half cup of pickling salt with one-half cup of aluminum sulfate, potash alum, or ammonium alum in one gallon of water. The salt-acid solution is made by combining one pound of salt and four ounces of sulfuric acid in one gallon of water.

Immerse the fleshed skin, let it set overnight, and the next morning remove the skin from the solution and peel off the membrane which should have loosened in the tanning solution. Use a knife to start the membrane around the hip areas of the skin. Then return the skin to the solution and let it soak for four to sixty days, stirring it often. The tanning is complete when the skin has turned an even color. If in doubt, leave the skin for an additional day or two, since it will do no harm.

After the tanning solution has done its work, remove the skin and rinse it very well in several changes of clean water. It also should be neutralized by using any of the acid-neutralizing solutions listed under tanning formulas. Oil and soften rabbit skins in the customary way.

4

Making Buckskin

I have hunted deer in several different states and probably have bagged more than 100 in about thirty-five years of hunting. Every pound of meat was eaten and every skin from these deer was either sold to a tannery or utilized at home. In the last few years, I have started making my own pipes and buttons from antlers, knife sheaths from the green leg skin, fishing lures from the tails, and several different articles of clothing from the skins. Buckskin is about the easiest of all leather to tan, but even so it requires quite a bit of work.

SKINNING THE DEER

The first step is to remove the skin without punching holes in the hide with the knife point. Usually bullet holes will not damage the skin to any great extent, but if you have a choice, put the bullet hole in the deer's neck. Then the large areas of the skin can be fully utilized without piecing it together. Although they are almost never available anymore, it is interesting to note that summer deer hides are thicker than winter hides. Some of the thickness of the hide is actually used in producing

The whitetail deer probably yields the most useful skin of any wild animal. The skin is also very easily tanned by many different processes.

the dense, hollow hair that makes up the deer's winter coat. Also, if a hide is to be tanned with the hair on, the summer coat which is reddish brown is more colorful and less apt to break off than grey winter hair.

The softest buckskin comes from a doe or young buck, and soft buckskin is most useful for making shirts and pants. The thick skins from an old buck are most useful for making moccasins; the skin taken from an old buck in the summer was probably what the Indians used for making their moccasins.

Deer are fairly large animals, but most people are surprised when they find out how many skins it takes to make a garment. For instance, a jacket requires four to five large hides; a pair of trousers, four hides; and even a shirt requires three large hides. Moccasins will take about ⅓ of a large skin, and gloves are often made from the scraps left after a large project has been cut out.

Deer are easy animals to skin since there is a good layer of fat separating the hide from the meat. However, I left a large buck hang until a week after the end of deer hunting season one year. During the last seven days, the weather got far below zero at night and the animal was rock hard by the time I got around to skinning him. I finally had to make up some wooden wedges to drive between the hide and the meat so I could get it off.

Since then I have skinned them as soon as possible. A deer that is still warm (within two hours after shooting it) is very easy to skin. About the fastest way to skin one is to hang it up by the neck and slit up the belly to the head, cutting around the neck skin. Cut off the front legs at the knee and the hind legs at the hock. Make a slit inside each leg to join the belly cut, and start skinning the legs, although there is no need to skin out the legs completely. Then start removing the skin around the neck, pulling it down until you have a loose flap of skin on the back of the neck.

Put a small rock or even a marble on the inside of the neck skin and tie a stout rope around it so the rock forms a bunch that will keep the rope from slipping off. Now tie the other end of the rope to an automobile bumper and back slowly away. This will pull the hide completely off the animal with little effort. The main disadvantage of this method is it is apt to leave a lot of flesh and fat on the hide.

Deer can also be skinned completely by hand; begin by hanging the deer up and making the belly and neck cuts as described earlier. Usually the skin can be pulled loose from the neck by gripping it with the hands. Strip the hide down towards the body using the knife only to keep large amounts of fat and meat from coming off with the hide.

When you reach the shoulders, cut off the front legs at the knee and slit up the inside of each leg to the belly cut. Skin out the legs to the body by pulling on the skin, using the knife sparingly. Then pull down on the neck skin to continue peeling the hide off the body. It usually peels pretty easily down the body, but before you get to the hips, cut off the hind legs at the hock and make a cut up the inside of the legs to the belly cut. Start the hide peeling off the legs, then go back to the body skin and pull it down until it comes off the hind legs. The tail will have to be cut off at the root to free the hide.

An abundance of tallow and flesh usually comes off with the skin. This has to be removed before the hide is salted and the best way to do it is to flop the skin hair side down on a fleshing beam, find a large two-handled fleshing knife, and start scraping. At this stage, be sure to remove all the large chunks of tallow and meat. I found that a deerskin can be fleshed very easily if it is placed in a freezer until the tallow just starts to freeze. This takes a surprisingly long time, and it is better to leave it slightly too long since it will thaw quickly if it freezes too hard before you start fleshing it. Of course, at this time there is no need to scrape it completely clean since it will be fleshed again and again during the process.

Skin the deer very carefully so there are no extra knife cuts. Probably the easiest way to do this is to hang the deer up first.

Almost the only time the knife needs to be used is around the legs and neck. Most of the rest of the skin can be pulled off or pounded loose by pulling on the skin with one hand and striking it with the other fist.

and flesh and be sure to remove the membrane that lays next to the hide. From experience I would say that the entire hide should be gone over at least three times. This isn't exceedingly difficult because a skillful operator can flesh a hide in less than fifteen minutes. Whatever extra time is spent on the hide will result in a better tanning job.

The next step in making buckskin is to remove the hair, and this is done by soaking it in a liming solution. Dehairing solutions are made from lime and water, ashes and water, or lye and water. Probably the easiest solution to work with is the lime and water mixture. Simply mix two pounds of (common) lime to twelve gallons of water for one deer hide, but if several hides are to be dehaired at the same time, mix eight pounds of lime to fifty gallons of water in a barrel. Put the hides in the solution and weight them down if necessary so all parts of the hide are covered in liquid.

The hides are left in the solution until the hair is very loose. This will take from four days in warm weather to two weeks in cold temperatures. When the hide is properly dehaired, the hair will slip when rubbed with heel of the hand. Long before this stage the hair can be pulled out by hand, so be sure to let it go long enough. Use rubber gloves when handling all tanning solutions.

When the dehairing solution has done its work, remove the skin from the solution, hang it to drain for a few minutes, and then start removing the hair. This is done by placing the skin flesh side down on a fleshing beam and using the back of the blade to scrape the hair off the skin. If the dehairing has been done properly, the hair and the hair roots will slough off when the skin is scraped with the back of the fleshing knife. Scrape the hide very well during this process to remove dirt, lime, and grease. Place a large section of plastic sheeting under the tanning beam and the hair can be picked up in it after you are done. An apron is needed to keep your clothes clean and dry. I use a plastic garbage bag tied around my upper waist for an apron.

BATING THE SKIN

Next the hide must be soaked to remove the lime from the skin since this will adversely affect the tanning process. This process is called bating and the first step is to wash the hide thoroughly in cool, clean water for at least eight hours. If the hide can be immersed in a tank and a water hose run into the tank so the water is slowly being changed, do this; otherwise, put the hide in a large container and change the water at least twice during the eight hours. Next dump out all the water from the barrel, and rinse out all of the sediment. Then refill the

SALTING THE SKIN

After it is fleshed, weigh it and lay it hair side down on
surface. Pour salt on the hide in the equivalent amount of one
of salt for each pound of hide, but use at least three pounds o
Probably the easiest way to do this is to pour the salt along the
of the hide from the tail to the neck area, and then spread it ou
rub it into the hide very well. Then fold the hide in half, roll it up
set it aside with one end slightly elevated so the moisture can
out of it. In two to four days, unroll the hide, shake out the salt, s
off any accumulation, and then resalt it again using a pound of sa
each pound of hide. Reroll the hide and leave it for two to four
days. Then if you won't be tanning it right away, spread it out fla
let it dry. It is better to stretch the hide and tack it down to a
surface so it won't shrink and wrinkle while it is drying. Be su
keep it out of the sun, rain, and excess heat if it is to be stored
quite awhile.

A dried deer hide is almost as stiff as a sheet of plywood a
requires special handling when the time comes to continue tannin
Be sure not to bend it if it is dry as this will cause a weak place in
leather and it may even crack clear through. Instead, mix up a solu
of ten gallons of water and ten ounces of borax and soak the hid
it. Sometimes the hide can't be fitted into a container because it is
stiff. In that case, sprinkle the solution on the flesh side of the hi
cover the hide with cloths, and let it set overnight. By the next morni
if not sooner, the hide will be flexible enough to fit into a tanning bar
without bending a stiff section of it.

The salted deer hide should be soaked in the borax solution
about two days. During this time it should be stirred at least twice
day to make sure the solution penetrates each section of the hide. Wh
tanning buckskin, you don't have to concern yourself with the pos
bility that the hair will start to slip because it will be removed anywa
When it is soaked long enough, the flesh and fat are easily remove
One way to tell if it is done is to scrape a section with a knife blac
before you remove it completely from the solution. If the fat seems t
be soft and easily removed, take the hide out of the solution and han
it up to dry for ½ hour or so to prevent the water from soaking you
clothing.

FLESHING AND DEHAIRING THE HIDE

When the moisture has mostly run out of the deer hide, lay it hai
side down on the fleshing beam and scrape off every last scrap of fat

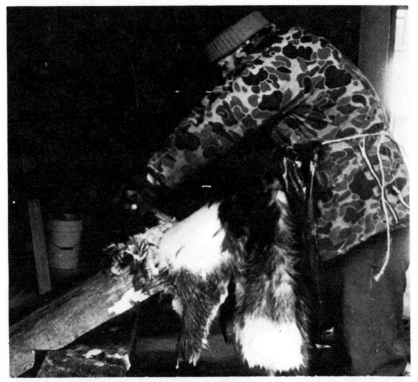

When the hair is loosened very well, drain the skin, put it on the fleshing beam, and scrape away the hair with the back of the fleshing knife. A properly prepared skin can be dehaired in ten minutes or less. It also should be refleshed at this time.

barrel, and add one ounce of lactic acid for each eight gallons of water, stirring it well. If lactic acid is not available, use one pint of vinegar to each eight gallons of water, and leave the hide in the solution for twenty-four hours, stirring it frequently. Then remove the hide, drain it, and scrape it on both sides to remove the lime that has been brought to the surface of the skin. Finally put the hide in clean water and let it soak again for twenty-four hours. When you take it out of this last bath, scrape it again on both sides with the fleshing knife, rinse it thoroughly, and it is ready for pickling.

CHROME TANNING THE DEER HIDE

Before a hide is chrome tanned, it is usually pickled to insure maximum effectiveness of the tanning solution. Although this step is sometimes eliminated by the home tanner, much better and longer lasting leather will be a result of pickling before chrome tanning, and it is practiced by commercial tanneries. Sulfuric acid, oxalic acid, or white vinegar can be used for pickling the skin. To make the sulfuric acid pickle, dissolve ½ ounce of pure sulfuric acid or two ounces of automotive (thirty-three percent) sulfuric acid and fourteen ounces of salt in each gallon of water. Oxalic acid is used in the amount of one ounce to each gallon of water also. White vinegar (five percent acetic acid) is used in the amount of two quarts of vinegar to each pound of skin and each pound of salt.

Both sulfuric acid and oxalic acid are dangerous. Use extreme care not to breath the fumes or splash any of the liquid on your bare skin. White vinegar is perfectly safe but expensive. When mixing the acid solution, first dissolve the salt in the water and then slowly pour the acid in the saltwater. Always wear eye protection and rubber gloves when working with acids. The pickling solutions can be reused, but when you dispose of them, be sure it is in a safe place.

Place the dehaired, scraped skin in the solution and make sure it is covered. Let it soak for twenty-four hours, stirring it often, to swell and soften the skin. After twenty-four hours, remove the hide and rinse it in clear water. If you want to leave the hide in the pickle longer than twenty-four hours, no harm will come to it. I pickled a beaver skin for three months once with no harm. However, before it is tanned, the skin should be rinsed and soaked overnight in clear water to remove the pickle solution.

A deer hide can be tanned by several different methods, and it will yield a useful product. Chrome tanning is considered the best way to tan a deerskin for garment use. When using chrome and sodium carbonate crystals together, the materials must be mixed at least forty-eight hours before use. This process is described in other chapters. For tanning this deerskin, finely ground chrome powder will be used that dissolves quickly. The chrome will be buffered after the penetration of the skin is complete by neutralizing it in sodium bicarbonate. Chrome crystals are acidic and poisonous, so always wear rubber gloves and eye protection.

After the skin is taken from the pickle and rinsed, let it drip until most of the water has run out of it. Then weight it (a large skin will weight about ten pounds), and mix up the chrome solution using one quart of 100° F. warm water and three ounces of chrome tan powder for each pound of hide. Stir this well and set it aside. Then mix eight ounces of salt and one gallon of water together for each pound of hide, and when the salt is dissolved, put the skin in the solution and let it soak for half an hour. Then remove the skin and pour half the chrome solution into the saltwater, stirring it very well. Replace the skin in the tanning liquid, make sure it is immersed, and let it soak for twelve hours while stirring and turning the skin. After twelve hours, remove the skin and pour the rest of the solution in the container. Put the skin back in and let it soak for four to five days, stirring it four times a day until the skin is evenly colored all the way through.

No harm will come to the skin from leaving it longer. Cut off a sliver of skin, and examine it to see if the tannage has fully penetrated the skin. It is also wise to double check this by boiling the sliver of skin for a few minutes to see if it stays intact. Untanned skin will harden and curl up, while tanned skin won't change very much in appearance.

After the tanning is complete, rinse the skin very well in clear water, and then neutralize the tanning solution by immersing the skin in a mixture of one ounce of bicarbonate of soda with each gallon of water. It will probably take eight to ten gallons of water to cover the skin. Soak the skin for two hours, plunging it up and down and stirring it frequently; then rinse it in three changes of clear water.

Dispose of the chrome solution when you are through (it shouldn't be reused) in a safe place. It will kill vegetation and animals if poured into a stream or river or lake. It will probably stratify a rural septic tank also.

Now the hide can be oiled and softened. First squeeze or slicker out the excess water from the skin, and then coat it on the flesh side with warm neat's-foot oil and let it dry. Just before it is completely dry—when you can bend a piece and it shows a white line—the hide is ready to be softened. While it is drying, pull the hide in all directions. Then when it is ready, stake it or put it in the clothes dryer with a clean tennis shoe and run the dryer until the hide is softened. Remember this hide will be thicker and somewhat stiffer than the split hides returned to the hunter by commercial tanners.

When the hide is staked, every inch should be gone over several times by pulling it over a staking edge. It has to be kept damp while this process is taking place; so if it dries, sprinkle warm water on it or roll damp towels against the flesh side until the hide becomes damp.

DYEING AND FINISHING

Chrome-tanned skins are usually dyed since the blue-green color of the tanning solution is not appealing to most people. The best dyeing

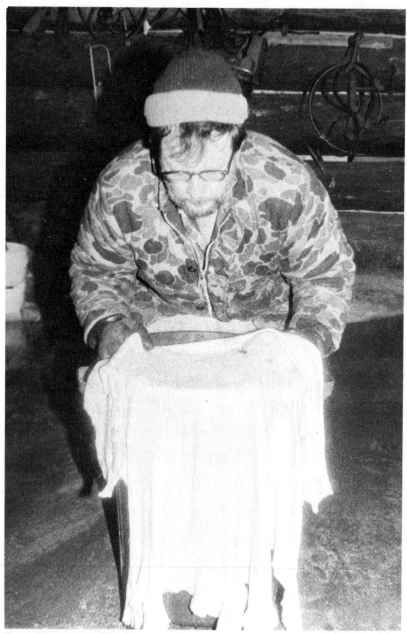
The tanner inspects a deerskin that has just been taken out of the tanning bath. The skin is clean, soft, and smooth and will make fine garment material.

method I have ever found is to immerse the skin in a dye bath made by steeping hemlock or oak bark in water.

Collect about two gallons of oak or hemlock bark in a plastic pail, and then pour two gallons of water, heated to the boiling point, over the bark. Let this mixture steep for at least two days or until it doesn't appear that the water will get any darker. Then strain the liquid through a cloth or sieve to remove the bark bits.

Heat the dye water to the boiling point, and let it stand until it starts to cool. Then immerse the deerskin in the dye, and stir it up very well to remove all the air bubbles from the skin. It should sink completely, but if it doesn't, place some weight on it so it's immersed. After the skin is in the dye for twenty-four hours or longer, remove it and rinse off the excess dye. The skin is now permanently dyed. Commercial dyes are also widely available from shoe shops, leather outlets, and taxidermy supply houses.

When the hide is as soft as you can make it, dampen it again and apply one pint of neat's-foot oil to the flesh side. If it is thick and stiff in some places, the hide can be thinned by rubbing it with sandpaper or a cloth dipped in pumice stone. Finish by rubbing it with neat's-foot oil or dubbin.

INDIAN-STYLE BUCKSKIN TANNING

Chrome-tanned leather is resistant to moisture and permanently preserved, but satisfactory buckskin can also be made with soap to

A large buckskin that has been chrome tanned and softened until it feels like good cloth.

produce a modern version of the Indian method of making buckskin. Skin the animal and let the hide lay overnight to cool out.

The next morning, mix up a solution of ¼ cup of lye dissolved in ten gallons of water. Soak the skin for twenty-four hours or until the hair will easily slip when a section is rubbed with the heel of the hand. Be sure to wear rubber gloves when working with a tanning solution.

When the hair is slipping well, remove the skin from the lye water, drain it for a few minutes, and then flop it on the fleshing beam and dehair it as previously described. At this time be sure to flesh the other side of the hide, removing every bit of flesh and fat and membrane that would restrict the action of the tanning liquid. If you have no other equipment, fleshing can be done using a butcher knife with the point driven into a hardwood block so that it forms a double handle for a fleshing knife. Almost any rounded surface, or even the top of a table, can be used as a fleshing beam. Be sure to remove the black and spongy layer of skin that the hair sets in; this is easy to remove if the dehairing process was done correctly.

Next, rinse out the soaking barrel and add ten gallons of water and two cups of vinegar to it. Replace the hide in the water and let it sit overnight to dilute and remove the lye water from the hide. The next morning, remove the hide from the barrel, dump it out, and rinse the hide thoroughly to remove all of the vinegar solution. It should be rinsed in three changes of water, squeezing and working the skin in the water with the hands to be sure it is thoroughly worked out.

Now the actual tanning can begin. Make up the tanning solution by dissolving two bars of naptha soap and a pint of neat's-foot oil in a cup of hot water. Add the dissolved soap to three gallons of hot water, and let it cool so you can hold your hand in it. Then put the hide in the tanning liquor, add clean water if needed, and make sure it is completely covered. Let it soak for three days, stirring it at least twice a day during this time. On the fourth day remove the skin from the solution, and hang it up for a few minutes until some dry spots show up on the hide. Then put it over a fleshing beam and scrape it on both sides with the back of the fleshing knife until it is dry.

Again return it to the tanning solution and let it set in the tanning liquor for another three days, stirring it as before. Then remove it from the liquid, wring it out to remove most of the moisture, and work it over a fleshing beam again. This process should make soft buckskin from the skin. If it appears unevenly stretched in some places so that it creates pockets, dampen the hide, lace it into a stretching frame, pull it taut, and let it dry. It should dry evenly. Then work it over a staking board to soften it.

Smoking a soap-tanned deerskin. This procedure is interesting but somewhat time consuming. The hide should be repositioned every hour or so and it will take at least one day to smoke it well.

This type of buckskin can be smoked to give it a pleasing color and odor and to make sure it will resist hardening after it gets wet. Smoke the hide until it is a golden brown, but make sure the smoking never raises the skin over a comfortable temperature to the touch. The actual smoking can take place outside by making a small tepee frame of branches, building a very small fire underneath it, and smothering the fire with damp alder or hardwood chips to produce an abundance of smoke. The skin is then draped over the frame and left to absorb the smoke until it is all an even color. This will take two or three days of intermittent smoking and turning the skin so it is all colored evenly.

5

Tanning the Large Furbearers

To my way of thinking, the large canine furbearers such as fox, coyote, and wolf are among the most beautiful animals on the earth. They are intelligent, possess superb physical agility and stamina, and are truly wild animals whether they are in a cage at a zoo or moving through their natural world.

TANNING FOX FUR

Foxes have fascinated men since before recorded history, and the ancients thought they possessed all sorts of super reasoning ability and cunning. One biblical story even tells how Sampson set fire to the fur of foxes and let them run through the high grass to route the Philistines. Incidently, this account resulted in a woolly phase of red fox called Sampson's fox because its coat lacks guard hairs and looks like it has been burned.

The red fox is found in Europe, and the colonial English sportsmen imported red fox to the southeastern part of the United States because the native grey fox would not run ahead of the hounds without ducking

Red foxes doze in a field in northern Wisconsin. Red fox fur is very valuable and easily tanned.

into a hole or running up a tree. Although for a time biologists believed the red fox was an immigrant from Europe, the bones of foxes eventually discovered in ancient pits proved that the red fox was in America long before the English came.

Fox is an extremely silky and luxurious fur, and when long-haired furs are in style, it commands the highest prices. This good price is maintained partially because of the difficulty of catching wild foxes. If you have a good fox hound and live in good fox country, you can probably get from 40 to 100 a year. Most of the foxes trapped are caught in a "dirt hole set" and this offers the best chance for a home tanner to obtain a fox skin for tanning.

First obtain a #1.75 steel trap and equip it with a steel drag or stake. If it is new, boil it in lye water for twenty minutes to remove the packing oil and hang it in a tree where it can get rained on. Leave it there until it is covered with a thin coat of rust, which shouldn't take more than two weeks. Now find a large metal can that will hold two gallons of water or more and half fill it with oak bark, walnut shells, or sumac bark. Add enough water to cover the bark, and put the rusted trap in the container. Finally, build a fire under the container and simmer it until the vegetable matter dyes the trap a dark brown or black. After it is stained, let the fire go out and leave the trap in the dye overnight so that the dye will set. Without touching the trap with your bare hands, take it out of the dye and hang it in a tree away from smoke or pollution and leave it there while you assemble a small tiling spade, about a half dozen small bits of half rotten meat or fish for bait, a box of facial tissue, and a foot square section of wire mesh or a trappers sieve.

Assuming that you have previously found a trail or food source where foxes have made tracks quite often, put on a pair of clean gloves, pick up the trap and other paraphernalia, and put them in a clean pail for easy carrying. Go to the site where the trap will be set and dig a hole twelve inches deep and four inches in diameter at a 45-degree angle. With the dirt piled on one side, dig out a bed for the trap in front of the hole, set the trap, and place it in this bed. The drag or stake is placed under the trap. Carefully cover the trap with two thickness of facial tissue and sift dirt over it until it is completely hidden.

Next put the rotten meat down in the hole and sprinkle a little bit of dirt over it so it won't be taken by birds. If you have a little fox urine, sprinkle about two drops in the back of the hole. Carefully spread out any loose dirt left around the hole and smooth out any tracks that you have made. If this was done correctly you will probably catch a fox within one day to two weeks.

The proper way to kill a fox in a trap is to tap him across the muzzle with a stout stick to knock him out. Then put your foot on the fox's chest for about five minutes to stop his heart. Now take the fox home and brush out all dirt and sticks from his coat. If it was killed correctly there shouldn't be any blood, but if it does bleed, wash this off with soap and water and hang it up by the muzzle to dry.

Skinning the Fox

When it is dry, skin by the case-skinning method which starts by making a cut up the inside of the hind legs. Skin out the base of the tail, pull the bone out, cut around the anus and genitals, and pull the skin off the hind legs and down over the body to the front legs. Pull the front legs out of the skin like pulling a finger out of a glove, leaving both front and rear paws on the skin. Skin the paws out to the toes and cut the toes off from the inside leaving the toes and claws on the skin. The head is completely and carefully skinned out with particular attention to the ears and eyes so no large holes are left there.

Fleshing the Skin

Foxes are considered easy to skin, but as soon as the hide is off it should be fleshed very well. The tanning should commence immediately for the very best chance at a good tanning job.

If the fox skin has been dried or if it is extremely hard to flesh, swab it on the flesh side with a solution made by dissolving one ounce of borax in one gallon of water. However, don't oversoak the skin since fox skins break down rapidly and hair slippage can occur. Then finish fleshing it and rinse it very well.

Tanning the Hide

Fox skin is thin and will tan very well by several different methods. An alum tan will be satisfactory for a wall trophy or rug. Find a container that will hold at least three gallons of water and weigh out three pounds of alum, three cups of salt, and twelve ounces of washing soda. Put three gallons of hot water in the container and add the solid ingredients, stirring them vigorously. When they are all dissolved, put the fox skin in the mixture and weight it down with a clean stone so the liquid covers it completely. Stir it at least four times the first day and twice a day for the next two days. In three days the skin should be completely tanned, but to make sure slice a section from the edge to see if the entire thickness of the skin has turned the same color.

After it is completely tanned, remove the skin from the tanning liquid and neutralize the tannage by soaking it for one hour in a bath made by dissolving three ounces of baking soda in three gallons of water. Rinse it well in clean water and squeeze out the excess; dry the hair with a fan, hair dryer, or vacuum cleaner, or by hanging the skin outdoors. When this is done, swab the flesh side of the skin with commercial tanning oil or a half and half mixture of sulfonated tanning oil and warm water. While the skin is drying, it will shrink unless it is pulled by hand or put back on the stretcher. It also can be slit down the belly and tacked out on a board, hair side up, to dry; in either case, be sure to stretch the tail. Stake or tumble the fox skin to soften it.

The gray fox is similar to the red, but it tends to be somewhat smaller and has slightly different habits. For instance, it has a much smaller range, spending its time in a small area of thickets and high grass. The gray fox can climb trees and often dens in a hollow log or rock pile; the red usually digs its den. Gray fox fur is not quite as luxurious as red and therefore it isn't as valuable. Gray fox is skinned and tanned like red fox.

TANNING COYOTE FUR

The coyote is also a well-known canine, with its intelligence surpassing even that of the fox. It is highly adaptable and can live nearly anywhere, though it probably prefers the western plains. Where I live in northern Wisconsin we hear the coyote nearly every night; its wild howling and barking seem to make the huge, silent forests surrounding our cabin come alive. We hunt and trap for them every year and usually manage to get a few, although they are extremely wary and innovative in evading traps and hunting ambushes. A man lives nearby who runs coyote with big white dogs, and when the snow conditions are just right, he is more successful than anyone else.

People who study the natural history of the coyote have unearthed some startling facts. One is the family life of the coyote and the care that both parents lavish on the young. Coyotes mate for life or at least for a long time, and the male brings food to the female when she is caring for the young. When she can leave them alone for awhile he might babysit or help her hunt for food for them. If something should happen to the female after the pups are weaned, the male will continue to feed and train them to maturity.

Another startling fact is the coyote's willingness to immigrate to other territories. When a pup is leaving home he might go 100 to 300 miles to another territory before he finds a place to his liking. If food gets scarce in their area, a pair might move for 50 to 100 miles and end up inside a large city, on a desert, or in a wooded area. They can survive in almost any environment.

Trapping the Coyote

The coyote is harder to trap than the fox, but the dirt hole set that was described for trapping fox is probably the most effective. You must use a larger trap though, either a #2 coil spring or larger; some trappers use the #4 double spring with good results. However, if you aren't experienced with hunting or trapping, I suggest you contact the local Department of Natural Resources office for the names of trappers in the vicinity and buy a coyote skin from one of them.

Skinning the Coyote

The coyote is extremely hard to skin because almost every inch of the hide is tight and must be worked off the body. Coyotes are case skinned like the fox. If you are going to use the coyote fur for a wall decoration, then the feet are skinned out; if they will be made into an article of clothing, the hide is cut off at the knee. Coyote hide is thicker than fox skin, and the hair is thicker and warmer. Comb the hair to remove burs and dirt lumps before you flesh it; lumps in the fur will cause the skin to be cut when it is fleshed.

The author's son catches coyotes, tans their skins, and sells them to tourists for wall hangings.

Coyotes are case skinned; they are hard to skin until the skinner has some experience.

When you have the hide removed from the body it can be fleshed, which is also a tedious job since the fat and flesh seem to stick to the hide.

If you don't want to tan it immediately, the hide can be salted, frozen, or dried by the same method that trappers use when they are preparing the hide for sale to a fur buyer. First find a suitable coyote stretcher or make one, and then turn the skin flesh side out and pull it on the stretcher. Tack it down at the crotch, at both legs on the underside, and at the base of the tail on the upper side. Spread the tail out and tack it down so it lies open and it won't spoil. Leave the hide on the stretcher until the skin has a glazed look, which means it has started to dry. Then remove the hide from the stretcher, turn it fur side out, put it back on, and tack it down in the same way as before. Don't remove the hide until it is completely dry, which will probably take about two weeks. It will keep this way for months if kept out of the sun and away from predatory insects, animals, or birds.

Trying to bend a coyote hide that is well dried will certainly make it break or weaken in several places; so soften the coyote hide by soaking it in water before handling it very much. It is usually best to add a teaspoonful of household bleach to each three gallons of water used to soak the skin. Remove the skin from the bath as soon as possible; it should relax after one to four hours of soaking.

Although several types of tannage will be satisfactory for coyote skins, the chrome tanning method will be described. First pickle the skin by immersing it in a sulfuric acid pickling bath. To make up the solution, weigh the soaked skin and for every pound of skin, add one gallon of water, four ounces of automotive-type sulfuric acid, and one pound of salt together. Dissolve the salt in the water, and then very slowly add the acid. *Caution:* Sulfuric acid is very dangerous if not handled correctly; so pour it slowly. Keep fresh water on hand and if you spill acid on yourself or get it in your eyes, spash water on it immediately.

Immerse the coyote skin and soak it for seventy-two hours or longer. Stir it often and keep the skin completely submerged by weighting it.

After the prescribed time, remove the skin from the sulfuric acid pickle and dispose of the pickle liquid. Wash out the container and add one gallon of water and eight ounces of salt to the container for each pound of coyote skin as previously weighed. In another container, dissolve three ounces of chromium sulfate crystals in one quart of water for each pound of skin. Immerse the skin in the saltwater and let it soak for half an hour, and then remove the skin and pour half the chrome solution into the saltwater and stir it well. Put the skin back in the solution, making sure it is all covered, and let it soak for twelve hours, stirring it well every three hours. Then remove the skin, and pour the rest of the chrome into the tanning solution. This time let it soak for two to five days, or until the blue tannage color has penetrated the skin.

When it is done, remove the skin from the tannage, rinse it well, and soak it for two hours in a neutralizing solution made by dissolving one ounce of baking soda in each gallon of fresh water. Remove and proceed to oil the skin as described for fox fur.

Coyote skins have to be staked to soften them. If two people are interested in the project, a good way to stake a large fur is to nail a 1- × -4-inch board to a tree or wall at about shoulder height with the staking edge upward. Place a support under the outermost end of the board. Standing on opposite sides of the board, the two people grasp the skin and scrape it back and forth across the staking edge to soften it. It is coated with neat's-foot oil periodically during the staking process and the ends of the hide are reversed about every twenty minutes. The skin can be staked by one person but it is more difficult. Large fur skins can also be tumbled in an automatic dryer with the heat turned off or in a barrel mounted on pulleys so it can be turned by an electric motor.

TANNING OTTER AND FISHER SKINS

Otter and fisher skins are nearly the same in thickness and texture: they both have tough, thick hides and soft, luxurious fur. Both are extremely difficult to sew; perhaps the only use most home tanners would have for these skins is as wall hangings for trophy mounts. Just to have such a skin hanging on a den or trophy room wall is extremely interesting to outdoor-minded people; however, if several skins are made into a garment, it is sure to be long lasting.

Both of these large weasels are difficult to trap and hard to skin. The otter is almost entirely a water animal, only coming out of the water for brief forays across the country to another water course. This often takes place when the otter travels up a small stream until he gets to the origin of it. He then takes off across the country to another stream or lake, following that to a river.

Otters feed to a large extent on small fish, often chubs or suckers. Many naturalists claim that an otter can swim fast enough to catch a fish, and when they decide to pursue a particular fish, he will be caught and eaten.

Trapping an Otter

The surest way to catch an otter for tanning is to set a #330 or #220 body grip trap in the winter in a small stream. First find a place where the water is between one and three feet deep. Use enough dead poles less than two inches in diameter to make stakes to "fence off" the stream from both sides, leaving an opening in the center of the stream which will just fit the trap. This can be about eight inches wide if you use a #220-type trap or about twelve inches if you use a #330 size body grip trap.

Set the trap in the opening using one stake on either side to anchor it, and place a "dive" stick over the trap so that the otter can't swim over the top. The dive stick forces him to dive down through the trap which is set on the bottom.

Skinning the Otter

After you catch an otter, take him home, dry him out, and proceed to skin him. Otters are case skinned and they are very difficult to skin. The customary cuts are made along the inside of the hind legs and the tail is split underneath. The otter has a large muscular tail and the bone can't be pulled out like a raccoon or mink tail; it has to be slit to the tip and skinned out inch by inch. Very little of the otter's skin will slip off; it has to be loosened with a knife along its entire length. Be extremely careful not to cut holes in the skin, but if it happens, they can be sewn up after tanning.

After the hide is free from the body, it can be fleshed before it dries. Otters usually don't have much excess flesh, but what stays on the skin is very hard to remove. I use a sharp knife and extreme care, and I shave the flesh off rather than scrape it as is done with some other animals.

Soaking the skin in a gallon of warm water that has an ounce of washing soda or borax dissolved in it will also soften the flesh and fat and make it easier to remove. Let the skin soak for about two hours and then resume fleshing. Everything about an otter hide is tough, and the membrane is going to be hard to remove. For tanning a wall trophy, the head must be retained, so the flesh around the eyes and ears will have to be scraped off also.

After the pelt is fleshed, it can be soaked in salt brine or dry salted to open the pores of the skin so the tanning solution will penetrate better. First weigh the pelt and then rub in a pound of salt for each pound of hide. Be sure to use finely ground noniodized salt. Two cups of salt is about one pound. If you decide to soak the skin in brine, dissolve one cup of salt to each gallon of water and soak it for about eight hours.

If the otter skin is dried, it should be soaked in clear water for about two hours or as long as it takes to soften it. All soaking water should have a teaspoonful of bleach added to kill the bacteria so it doesn't attack the skin. Wet skins can be used without soaking.

Otter and fisher skins can be tanned by any of the processes described for fox or coyote, or they can be paste tanned. To paste tan a skin, slit it up the belly and tack it flesh side up on a stretching frame or board. Keep it from drying out completely by covering the flesh side with damp newspaper while you are mixing up the paste tan.

Mix one pound of aluminum sulfate or ammonium alum and one pound of salt together by pouring both ingredients in a container and stirring them with a spoon. In another container, dissolve three ounces of gambier in a cupful of boiling water. Add the gambier to the rest of the ingredients and also add enough hot water to saturate and dissolve the salt and alum. If the paste is too thick, add water; if it is too thin, add wheat flour. Regulate the paste so it can be spread on the skin with a trowel or stick.

Now lay out the skin flesh side up, smooth it out very well, and tack it down so it won't shrink and wrinkle during the process. When this is done, use a brush or your hands covered with rubber gloves to coat the flesh side of the skin with an ⅛-inch thick coating of the tanning paste. Cover the skin with plastic or similar material so it won't dry out. Leave it overnight, then scrape off the old paste and apply a fresh coat; both an otter and a fisher skin will require three coats. When the last coat is put on, leave the skin uncovered and let it start to dry out.

Keep an eye on the project, and when it has dried to the damp stage, take the hide off the stretching frame and wash off the flour paste. Mix two ounces of powdered borax with two gallons of water and soak the skin in this solution to neutralize the acid in the tannage and to clean the skin. After about two hours of soaking, rinse it well in several changes of clean water, or using running water.

Squeeze out the water by hand, put the skin on the fleshing beam, and use the slicker to push out most of the water. Return the skin to the stretching board or to another smooth flat surface, apply a thin coat of tanning or neat's-foot oil, and let the skin continue to dry while it absorbs the oil.

When it is just barely damp, take the skin off the stretching frame and start working it over the beam or stake. This is usually done by seesawing it over the edge of a board or a staking edge until it is soft.

If it dries out, apply a little more oil and continue working it. If it must be put aside for awhile, roll it up inside a damp cloth so it won't dry out too much. This will probably be a lengthy process, but it must be continued until the skin is soft and flexible.

After the beaming is done, the fur should be cleaned and all excess oil and dirt taken off the flesh side of the skin by rubbing sawdust into the skin. Then comb or brush it out of the fur and off of the skin side. If stiff spots remain they can be sanded or scraped to thin it down.

TANNING BEAVER FUR

The beaver is the very symbol of frontier and earlier 'trapper' eras. Superbly adapted for survival, the "flat tail" is the only animal that creates its own environment. It finds a suitable stream with tree-lined banks and builds a dam so that the water will spread out and create a pond right next to its favorite food trees. Then it cuts the trees down, eats the bark, and makes its lodge from the peeled logs and large branches.

The beaver pond provides a safe haven for the animals in summer and winter; it also provides a way to transport the logs from the bank to the house because the beaver either fells the trees into the water or digs canals from the water to the trees and thus is able to float the logs to its house.

Beaver are the largest rodents, often weighing up to 60 pounds; a few have reached 100 pounds in weight since they continue to grow for their entire lives. They are usually brown in color, but some are nearly black, and some colonies are made up of mostly all black animals. Beaver don't have prime skins until late winter.

Trapping the Beaver

Beaver are found in nearly all states where forests offer them food. They are easily trapped since they aren't particularly suspicious of traps. One good open water set which would be useful in the southern states is the castor set with a #4 double spring–leg hold trap. Find a place along the pond bank where the water is eight to twelve inches deep and adjoining an area where the water is about three feet deep. Use your boot to form a flat bed for the trap so it will be submerged about eight but less than twelve inches. The trap should have a long chain attached to it so it can be staked out from the bank in about three feet of water. The trap should either be weighted with a thirty-pound weight, or a double stake should be used so the animal will get

Beavers are fairly large animals, and often the trapper must drag them to the road from the remote ponds where they are caught.

tangled up in deep water and quickly drown. Beaver are extremely strong, and if they don't drown right away, they will pull the stake and get away with the trap.

In the north where the beaver lives under the ice in winter, he is successfully trapped under water with the bait set. First find a place on the beaver pond where the water is at least four feet deep. The closer you get to the house, the sooner the beaver will find the bait— a set close to the feed bed is sure to be noticed. Use aspen twigs about ¾ inch in diameter for the bait. Such twigs are a favorite food of the beaver and he is sure to investigate them since he is apt to eat his stored supply early in the winter.

After locating a place for the bait, cut a hole in the ice about eighteen inches long and one foot wide. After cutting bait into twelve-inch long pieces, you should have a bundle of twigs about six inches in diameter. Wire them into a bundle with mechanic's wire which is sold by trapping supply houses.

Next find a dead tree at least six inches in diameter. Cut off a ten foot piece and sharpen the upper end with an axe so it can be pushed into the bottom of the pond. Take the sharpened pole to the hole in the ice and push it in the hole and into the bottom of the pond as far as you can. Now make a mark on the pole where the water line comes, pull the pole back up again, and lay it down on the ice. Measure the depth of the ice and wire the bundle of twigs lengthwise to the pole so it will be at least one foot under the ice.

Set a #330 Conibear-type trap, place it over the bundle of twigs, and fasten the upper and lower springs to the pole. Now carefully pick up the pole and push it into the bottom of the pond so it will be secure for an hour or so until the ice freezes around the top of the pole.

Beaver traps are usually checked only twice a week, because if you chop into the set too often you can frighten the beaver so it won't come to the trap. However, sooner or later if the set is made correctly, you should catch one. Pull him up, take him home, and dry him out before you start skinning.

Skinning the Hide

A beaver is quite tedious to skin, but it doesn't take any particular expertise. Start by finding a location where the beaver can be laid on his back. He must not be frozen. You should be able to sit down on a chair while skinning since it will probably take nearly an hour to skin one beaver. Sharpen your skinning knife and keep it sharp.

First cut the legs off right at the bottom of the fur, which also

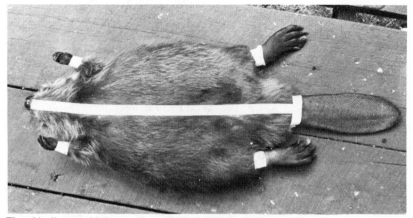

The white lines on this beaver show where the skinning cuts are made. The legs are removed before the skinning starts. The tail can be taken off or skinned out and left on the pelt and tanned along with the pelt when a wall hanging is going to be made.

happens to be the last joint. When all four legs are cut off, make a knife cut just under the skin from the tail up the center of the belly, coming out at the lower lip. You will have to cut around the anus on each side. A beaver is the only mammal that has only one opening for the anus and sex organs.

These are the only cuts you will make in the skin. Begin skinning with a flap of skin at the center of the belly and proceed by cutting every inch of skin loose from the fat. This process has been described as shaving, which comes very close to the truth. When the skin has been loosened on one side down to the back, go to the other side and do the same. Then turn the beaver on his side and skin the rest of the hide loose. The ears and eyes have to be skinned out carefully.

Fleshing the Skin

When the beaver hide is removed and laid out flat, it will resemble a huge, oval target. Although it has been carefully skinned, it will still need to be fleshed before tanning can start. Using the large fleshing beam and the fleshing knife, remove as must fat as possible. The smallest fleshing beam will be most useful for cleaning off the flesh and fat around the head.

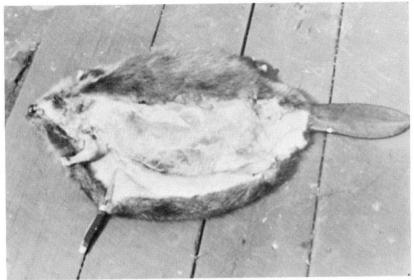

Beaver are skinned by shaving the hide away from the carcass starting from a line down the center of the belly.

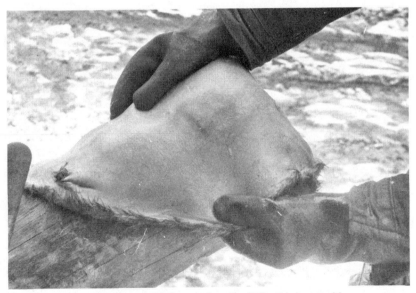

A properly fleshed skin is smooth and soft like this beaver skin.

Degreasing the Fur

Beaver skins are very greasy and need to be degreased before they are tanned, otherwise the tanning solution would be adversely affected. Flesh the skin to remove as much flesh and fat as possible, then pour two to three gallons of kerosene in a large container and immerse the beaver skin in the kerosene. Work and plunge it in the degreasing fluid for at least fifteen minutes. Let it soak for an additional fifteen minutes, work it again for about five minutes, and remove it from the kerosene.

After being degreased in kerosene, the skin should be washed in warm water and detergent. Mix up three gallons of hot water and three tablespoons of Tide or another strong detergent soap. Wash the skin very well in this detergent and then rinse the soap out by plunging the skin in a clear water bath, making sure all the detergent is removed.

Tanning the Hide

I made a fine wall hanging from a beaver skin by just pickling the skin after it was degreased. The customary sulfuric acid and salt mixture previously described was used for a tannage. I left the skin in the

Stretch the beaver skin into a hoop shape by tacking it to a board; using a screwdriver or similar tool, slide the skin up towards the head of the nail. The space between the hair and the board will allow the hair to dry quickly.

solution for four days, stirring it every day; then I took it out and neutralized the acid by soaking it for two hours in the bicarbonate of soda bath.

After it was neutralized, I rinsed the skin and dried the hair as quickly as I could. While the skin was still damp I swabbed tanning oil on the skin and stretched it in an oval shape on a plywood sheet. After the skin was dry and I took it off the stretcher, it laid flat and was properly shaped for a wall hanging.

Any other tanning process described could have been used on the beaver skin also. It could even be stretched after it was degreased and paste tanned right on the stretching board. Beaver skins are thick and would have to be shaved or sanded if they were going to be used for garments.

Any unusual or rare skin like this raccoon with a white cross on its back makes a fine wall hanging. It can be tanned for less than $3 and sold for up to $150.

TANNING RACCOON FUR

Raccoon is another larger furbearer that the home tanner will want to tan; raccoon skin hats, rugs, and wall hangings make fine additions to a den or cabin. Case skin the raccoon and then put it on the fleshing beam and flesh it very well. 'Coons are usually well coated with fat but it comes off easily. If you are going to keep the head, be sure to clean the flesh around the eyes and ears.

Raccoon skins also have to be degreased using the method described for the beaver hide before they are tanned. Then slit the skin down the middle to open it up and use the alum or sulfuric acid tan if the animal will be used for a wall hanging or rug. If desired, the chrome tan can be used for skins that will be made into garments. Alum-tanned skins can also be retanned with chrome if desired.

6

Tanning Moose and Elk Hides

Moose, caribou, and elk are the largest hoofed game animals in North America, and almost every hunter would like to bag such a trophy: most sportsmen are content with one in a lifetime. Since it will be a lifetime trophy, many men will have the heads mounted, but most of the skins are sold, given away, or just wasted. This is a pity since moose hide or elk hide make fine moccasins, robes, mittens, vests, leggings, shirts, jackets, parkas, and many other items. Tanning these hides is possible for most anyone with a garage or basement to work in.

SALTING THE FRESH HIDE

First, the skin should be well salted as soon as it is taken from the animal. It is wise to take salt with you on your hunting trip if you can manage it. As soon as the skin is removed and allowed to cool, the large pieces of tallow and meat are cut away and it is salted using one pound of salt for each pound of hide. If you have no scale, a cup of salt weighs about ½ pound and an average moose or elk hide will

Moose feeding in a northern lake.

weigh in excess of twenty pounds. Otherwise, just spread a good thick layer of salt over the skin, fold it in half, and roll it into a ball. If you can manage it, resalt it again in about three days, scraping off the old salt and drying the hide with grass or cloth if moisture stands on it. If the hide is so large it's hard to handle, split it in two pieces by cutting it down the backbone. It can be sewn back together if you want to make a robe from it.

Keep the hide in a cool place at all times, and it should be in very good condition when you get back home. The hide can be tanned with the hair on for use as a robe, Eskimo-type parka, wall hanging, or rug.

TANNING FUR

Cleaning and Fleshing the Skin

Before you start tanning, the skin should be soaked and scrubbed, especially if it is caked with mud and blood. Immerse it in clear water until it is relaxed, then scrub the hair with a stiff brush. Dump the first water and soak it again for two hours in a borax bath made by dissolving one ounce of borax to each gallon of water. Now that the hide is softened, it should be fleshed very well and washed again in clear water. Dump that water and let the hide dry overnight.

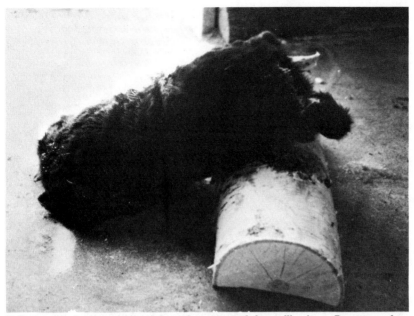

Roll up a salted skin by folding it in to the center and then rolling it up. Prop one end up on a log so the moisture can run out the other end.

Thinning the Hide

The next morning, lay the hide out on a flat surface and use a tanner's skiving knife to thin the hide. If possible, the entire hide should be reduced to ⅛ inch thick or less. This is done to make sure the tanning solution will penetrate it sufficiently and to make it soften easier. If you don't have a skiving knife, carefully cut shallow slits in the thickest part of the skin to aid penetration of the tanning solution. Then sand the hide after it is tanned to thin and soften it.

Paste Tanning the Fur

Either an immersion or paste tan will tan a skin with the hair on, but avoid oversoaking which might cause the hair to start slipping. A hide in good condition will stand the immersion tanning, but if any doubt exists, it is best to paste tan it.

The skin should be stretched on a drying frame or tacked on a sheet of plywood before the tanning solution is applied. Then it can be placed in a horizontal position so the solution won't run off when it is brushed on as a liquid. Whether the solution is applied as a liquid or paste, it should be kept covered so it won't dry out, and I find that plastic sheeting works well. Then the skin can be watched closely and an additional application can be made as soon as the previous one has soaked into the skin.

A good solution for paste tanning hair on skins is made by dissolving 2½ pounds of aluminum sulfate and one pound of salt in a gallon of soft water that has been heated to near boiling. Stir the ingredients until they dissolve and allow the water to cool before you put it on the hide. This can be brushed on the skin or it can be thickened with wheat flour and applied as a paste. Make up additional tanning solution as needed.

Keep applying the tanning solution to the hide until the tanning color penetrates the entire hide. This will take from four to ten days depending upon the thickness of the skin and several other factors. After the last application, the hide should be left uncovered.

Finishing the Hide

When the paste has dried, scrape if off and soften the hide by thinning and beaming it. A hide used for a wall hanging or rug doesn't need to be softened as much as a robe skin. Tanning oil is rubbed into the skin during the beaming process to aid in softening the skin. Most home tanners use a half and half mixture of tanning oil and warm water that is swabbed or brushed on the skin during the staking process.

Synthetic Tanning the Fur

Several of the synthetic tanning products used by taxidermists will tan an elk or moose skin with hair on and produce a skin that can be softened without undue problems. Probably one of the best is sold under the name of Kwik-Tan, but it is also more expensive than chrome tanning, and the tanner must decide if the extra expense is warranted. The chrome tanning process is described in chapter 9, but the Kwik-Tan process is as follows:

First relax and flesh the skin very well. Then it must be pickled, using either the sulfuric acid pickle or oxalic acid. Oxalic acid pickling solution is made by mixing one gallon of water, one pound of salt, and three level teaspoons of oxalic crystals together for each pound of hide (about fifteen gallons of solution). Immerse the skin, stir it well, and let it soak for at least twenty-four hours. It should change color slightly when the acid has fully penetrated. No harm will come from leaving the skin in the pickle after this stage, but don't remove it too soon.

When the skin is pickled, take it out of the solution and pour five fluid ounces of Kwik-Tan in the solution for each pound of skin. Stir it well and replace the skin. Allow it to remain in the solution until the skin has turned white all the way through, about forty-eight hours for a thick skin. When the skins are fully tanned, remove them from the solution and squeeze the excess moisture from them.

After the skin is taken out of the Kwik-Tan, the hair should be dried as fast as possible without drying out the skin. Drying the hair prevents it from slipping and in fact sets it permanently. Probably the fastest way to do this is to use a hair dryer or set a vacuum cleaner to the blow stage and blow warm air on the hair while you are brushing it until it is dry. The old-time method was to rub warm cornmeal or sawdust into the hair, hang the hide up, and pound it with a switch until the sawdust fell out again. Kitty litter is also a good product for drying and degreasing hair and fur. Some tanners also tumble the skin in the clothes dryer set at low heat for a few minutes until the hair is dry.

Finishing the Fur

The flesh must be kept damp so the oil will penetrate, which is the next step. First, lay the skin out hair side down on a clean, flat surface. A large table is ideal since it is at a convenient height for applying the oil. Mix half warm tap water and half tanning oil or sulfonated neat's-foot oil and swab the skin well with the mixture. Keep the oil from running on the hair by wiping the excess away from the edges of the skin. Let the skin set for eight hours or longer, and then apply another coat. A thick skin might absorb up to four coats of oil before it is saturated. After it won't absorb any more oil, wipe off the excess, and it is ready to dry.

Allow the skin to dry until it is just slightly damp, which will take up to eight hours for a thick skin. Then it can be beamed or tumbled to soften it. If equipment is available, skive the skin to thin any hard spots. After it dries, sand the flesh side to give it a smooth finish.

TANNING LEATHER

Cleaning and Fleshing the Hide

Many hunters will also want their hide tanned with the hair off to use as leather for shirts, jackets, or other articles of clothing. Start this process by soaking the hide overnight in clean water. When it is limp

The large hoofed mammals have amazingly thick hides. This skin from a moose is nearly ½ inch thick at the neck. The thick skin is used for shoe soles, belts, and scabbards. If it is used for clothing it must be thinned.

enough to handle, finish fleshing it, and wash it well if it is dirty or bloody. To wash an extremely dirty skin, I use one ounce of Tide detergent for each gallon of warm (100° to 120° F.) tap water. I let the skin soak for about one half hour and then plunge it up and down in the barrel with a rubber plunger (the kind used by plumbers for unstopping sinks and toilets); about ten minutes of this action will clean up nearly any skin. Then the soap must be dumped and the skin rinsed by plunging it again.

Dehairing the Skin

When the skin is clean, set it aside and mix up enough lime solution to cover the skin using one pound of hydrated lime for each five gallons of water. Put the skin in the solution and let it soak, moving it around every day until the hair is well loosened. When the hair is properly loosened (after six to ten days), it will come off in your hands when you attempt to lift the skin from the water.

When it is ready, lift it from the barrel and hang it on a beam or line to drain. Then flop it flesh side down on your fleshing beam and scrape the hair off. Make sure you scrape all the hair and hair roots off, and push hard enough to loosen and remove any crusted dirt. When this is done, turn the hide over and flesh it again to make sure any membrane or fat loosened by the last soaking is scraped off.

Deliming the Hide

The next step is to remove the lime water from the hide since this would adversely affect the tanning solution. Do this by thoroughly soaking the hide in lukewarm water, moving the hide around freely and changing the water twice to remove all loose lime. Finally, place the hide in the barrel, cover it with clean water, and add one ounce of lactic acid or a pint of vinegar to each twelve gallons of water. Let it soak overnight or for twelve hours, and then remove the skin, dump the solution, add fresh water, and rinse the skin very well. At this point it is ready for tanning.

Combination Tanning the Leather

Moose and elk hides are so rare that a hunter may want to tan his hide by the best possible methods so it will be as useful and long lived as it can be. Experts agree that a combination chemical and vegetable tan is superior to a tanning process that uses only one or the other.

When monitoring aids such as hydrometers, salinometer, thermometers, and pH indicators are available, the different solutions can be combined so only one bath is necessary. Since the home tanner will probably not have these to use, the chemical tanning process will be done first, followed by the vegetable tan. Because of the order of the processes, the skin is dyed brown after it has turned blue-green in the chrome-tanning process.

The first step in the chrome-tanning process is pickling the skin with oxalic or sulfuric acid. This has been covered in chapter 9, but a brief description will be repeated here. First mix up a solution consisting of two ounces of automotive battery sulfuric acid, one pound of salt, and one gallon of water for each pound of hide. Soak for at least twenty-four hours (longer soaking will not hurt) or until the skin has completely plumped up from the acid. Now rinse the skin and immerse it in a salt solution made by combining ½ pound of salt with one gallon of water for one half hour.

In the meantime, mix up three ounces of chrome crystals in a quart

A chrome-tanned elk hide, split.

of warm water for each pound of hide. Remove the skin from the salt solution, pour half the chrome solution in the salt mixture, stir it well, and replace the skin. Let it soak for ten to twelve hours stirring it well. Then remove the skin, add the rest of the chrome, stir it up, and replace the skin. This time let it soak, stirring it at least twice a day, for two to four days until the color has completely penetrated the hide. Then remove and rinse the hide, and immerse it in an alkaline solution made by dissolving one ounce of bicarbonate of soda in each gallon of water. Once the hide is well rinsed, it is ready for the vegetable-tanning process.

Gambier, terra japonica, suma extract, and a new vegetable tanning agent called Tannin-Blend (which is a by-product of the paper industry) will all finish tanning this hide and dye it as well. All require about one ounce for each pound of hide and each gallon of water required to make an immersion solution. The companies that sell these products furnish instructions for using each. However, there is no reason the home tanner can't produce his own vegetable tanning and dyeing solution to finish this project.

Make a fine dye and vegetable-tanning agent for the twenty-pound skin by chipping up enough hemlock or oak bark to fill a three–cubic foot container. Put it in a metal barrel, pour enough water over the bark to cover it, and place it over a fire and simmer it for about three hours. Then let it cool, strain the bark out of the water, and the vegetable tan is ready to use. Pour the solution in the tanning barrel and put the skin in, making sure it is all covered by weighting it down with stones if needed. Leave the skin in the solution, stirring it very well until the dark color has completely penetrated the skin. This will take from six to ten days, but much longer immersion will do it no harm.

Finishing the Leather

Once the hide is thoroughly tanned, take it out of the solution and wash it in four changes of clean water. After this cleaning, dissolve one pound of borax in twenty gallons of water and put the hide in, stirring it frequently. After it has soaked in the borax solution for twelve hours, dump it out and wash the skin for an entire day, changing the water five or six times.

After it is washed, dump the water and hang the skin over the beam to drain off, then proceed to "fat-liquor" or oil the hide to soften it. First stretch the hide out on a stretcher board or tack it out on a sheet of plywood with the flesh side outward. All loose folds should be pulled out of the hide and, in the case of thick leather, it should be gone over thoroughly with a slicker to push out most of the water.

Then apply a substantial layer of sulfonated neat's-foot oil to the flesh side. Leave the hide in the frame until it is dry then take it down and dampen it again with warm water until it is soft and pliable. Then apply a thick coating of warmed dubbin to the grain side of the leather. Make up the dubbin by melting together equal amounts of tallow and neat's-foot oil or cod-liver oil. When cool it must be soft and pasty but not liquid: if it is liquid add more tallow. Commercial tanning oil is also available.

After you apply the dubbin, restretch the hide, and let it dry. Then take the hide down, scrape off the dubbin with a slicker, dampen again, apply another coat of warmed dubbin, and restretch the hide. To finish, take it down and scrape off the dubbin again; rub the hide with sawdust to remove surface oiliness.

You don't have to tack the hide to a frame if you keep pulling and stretching it by hand as it dries. This can be done with your hands, leather-pulling pliers, or vise grip pliers with the jaws wrapped in tape. I have pulled both cattle and deer hides while they were drying by clamping one section of the hide in the vise and pulling on the other sections with pliers.

Each time the hide is taken from the drying frame it should be staked or tumbled to help soften it. If any type of tumbling device such as a clothes dryer is available, the hide can be tumbled to soften. Just be sure to leave the heat cycle off. The skin can also be hung up and pounded with a club or walked on to soften it. I have had the best luck by applying a thin layer of oil periodically during the softening process.

At this time you can determine whether you are going to use the skin for moccasins or for shirts: mocassin skin can be made much stiffer than shirt or garment skins. Softening the hide is one of the biggest problems associated with tanning thick leathers, but it can be done by patiently oiling and working the skin.

7

Tan Your Own Bearskin Rug

Black bear hunting is, to my way of thinking, the most thrilling hunt still available to the average person. To see a big black bear come into your bait station or running ahead of a pack of dogs is the stuff that dreams are made of. Perhaps that's why black bear hunting is getting more popular every year, especially since many states have developed bear management to a high degree and thus are able to keep a good-sized population of bears in the forest.

I have hunted bear for many years and seen many wary and elusive animals, especially the older ones who have been exposed to hunting pressure. However, this year I believe I saw the wariest of them all.

As usual, I started a bait station for bear early in August so the bear would find it by the time hunting season opened. Almost immediately I started getting "hits" which is bear hunter language for evidence that the bait is being eaten by bears. I took my shovel the next time and dug up fresh dirt and spread it around the bait so I could see what size the animal was. The next time I looked I could see bear tracks of a very respectable size around the bait. Good enough. I was

The black bear is an elusive game animal that is fully capable of self-defense if there is a need. His meat is tasty, and a bearskin rug is the heart's desire of many fireplace owners.

pleased with the developments and looked forward to bagging the animal early in the season since he seemed so interested in the bait.

To make a long story short, I hunted for the bear every day in the season, sitting in my tree stand for the first two hours in the morning and the last two hours in the afternoon. I never saw the bear even though he was taking bait about every second day. "A night feeder," I said to myself. I'd had them before. They come in only at night and thus are impossible to bag. Usually they have been shot at before or are bedding down so far away from the bait that they don't get there before shooting hours are over. Finally, the last day of the season, I went in the late afternoon to halfheartedly wait for the bear to come even though I had about given up. Too discouraged to even climb up to my tree stand, I just sprawled behind a deadfall where I could see the bait from the ground and half dozed in the warm September sun.

Just before dark I could hear very light footsteps on the forest floor with long pauses between them; then came a strange dragging noise. Waiting, I finally saw a black patch and a bear's uplifted ears.

It stood up and inched forward. This super-elusive creature was actually walking forward towards the bait for a few steps and then laying down on the ground, all the time keeping his nose testing the wind and his eyes examining the tree stand to see if I was up there. Clearly he knew where I usually waited for him and he had just about made up his mind that I hadn't come that day. However, when he stood up to make the last few inches to the bait he presented an easy shot.

Such an intelligent creature deserved to be remembered, I thought, so I decided to tan his hide. After checking with several commercial tanneries about the price of bear hide tanning I decided to tan his hide myself. I knew it would be alot of work—and it certainly was—but I feel the finished job was worth it.

SKINNING THE BEAR

The first step in tanning the bear hide is skinning it. Bears are field dressed when they are bagged so the skin is already slit up the belly. I could have hung the bear up and skinned him as I've done to several other bears, but I laid this one back down on a skinning bench; and when I had finished I decided that was a vastly superior way of skinning him, especially when an overhead hoist or rope is available to hold up part of the animal or to hold it in a certain position while the skinning is underway.

Although a bear can be skinned while hanging, I like to do it when it is laying on a bench at a comfortable working height.

Bear hide is tough so a sharp knife is necessary for making the cuts, but most any skinning knife will be equal to the task. I used my pocket knife with a three-inch blade and I kept a sharpening stone handy for touching up the blade whenever it started to get dull.

Laying the bear on his back, make the first cut, extending the field dressing up the center of the chest, along the neck and up the center of the lower jaw through the lips. Use the knife to skin back the edges of this cut so each side is laid back about two inches. Then make a skinning cut from the belly cut up the inside of each front leg and through the center of the front paws.

The next step is to lay the edges of the skin back from this front leg-skinning cut and skin out the paws. Skinning out the paws is probably the most difficult part of the bear skinning. I made sure the knife was sharp, and then I cut off the pad, removing all the pad skin and flesh. The foot bones make this difficult. Each one has to be removed and then the claws are cut off at the last joint and left on the skin. This must be done very carefully and all the flesh and foot bones must be taken out.

Continue skinning out the front legs using the knife to trim as much fat from the hide as possible as you skin. Keep the edge of the skin

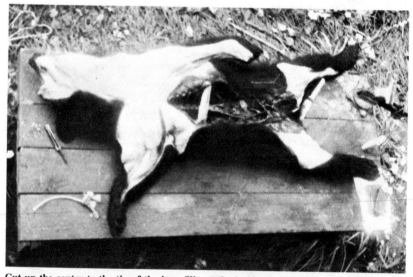

Cut up the center to the tip of the jaw. Slit up the inside of the legs and the center of the paws, and work the skin off. Bearskin can't be pulled off like deerskin; each inch has to be cut loose with the knife. It's easy to make skinning cuts, and extreme care should be used to avoid having to sew them up again.

folded back from the cut so it doesn't touch the meat and contaminate it; the meat is very good tasting and well worth preserving in its best condition.

When the front legs are skinned back to the body, go to the hind legs and slit the skin up the inside of both legs to the paws. Skin these out as you did the front paws, and then skin out the legs back to the body so that all four leg skins will be loosened.

Use the overhead ropes or blocks under the carcass to lean it in each direction so the skinning will be made easier. Keep skinning the hide off down to the back, being very careful not to make any cuts in

Skin out half the bear, then roll it over and skin out the other side. Keep it in position with wooden blocks.

the skin. When you can't skin any farther because the carcass is laying on the skin, roll it over on the right side and skin out the left side down to the backbone. Then roll it over to the left and skin out the right side, freeing the hide. The short tail is left on the hide and skinned out so it will take the tanning solution.

The neck is relatively long for an animal, but it skins easy. When you get to the head, be careful of skinning cuts as the skin is tight. Cut the ears off at the base and carefully trim around the eyes. Skin out the ears as much as possible by turning the ear skin inside out and peeling off the ear cartilage as you go. The lips also are left on the hide and they should be skinned out very carefully, removing the flesh from the inside of the black outer skin. Also, remove the cartilage from inside the nose.

After the skin is off the animal, roll it up, set it aside, and butcher the carcass into roasts, chops, and steaks and get it in the freezer immediately. Then unroll the hide and flesh off the large chunks of fat

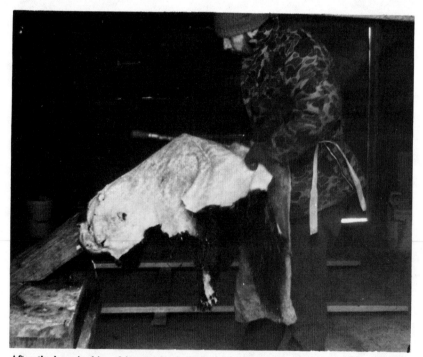

After the bear is skinned it must be fleshed very well. Be sure to scrape the leg skins and the flesh from the inside of the paws.

and meat that are left on the hide. If you have time, do a pretty thorough job of fleshing at this time. I like to flesh bear hides with a two-handled fleshing knife, starting from the rear and working towards the head. This is a considerable job and it should be done thoroughly so no part of the hide is left untouched. When you get to the head area you will have to use a knife or a fleshing tool with a fairly sharp blade to clean off the tight meat and fat.

SALTING THE HIDE

Once the bearskin is fleshed to your satisfaction, it is time to salt it down. First weigh the hide, and then weigh out that amount of salt in a pail or other container, as the ratio is one pound of hide to one pound of salt. The hide will probably weigh from ten to twenty pounds. I buy noniodized salt from the local farmers cooperative which costs about $3.50 for eighty pounds. It is ground fine and therefore penetrates better than coarse rock salt.

Lay the hide hair side down on a floor or even on the ground, and pour about half the salt in the center of the hide. Spread it out over the skin in a layer as far as it will go, and then distribute the rest to complete an even layer all over the hide. This first application should be rubbed into the hide very well, and there also should be free salt left in a thin layer over the entire hide to make up for any spots that were partially missed.

Next roll the hide up, hair side out by folding the sides into the center so they meet in the middle of the back. Then roll the hide from the head towards the tail. Set the hide on a slight incline so the water drawn out of the hide during this initial curing will run out. After two days in warm weather or four days in cool weather, unroll the hide. Lay it hair side down on a fleshing beam, and use the fleshing knife to scrape off the salt from the first application. Then resalt the hide using the same procedure as the first application. Roll it up again and leave it for two additional days.

After two days, you can start tanning the hide, or it will keep for several months without tanning. If you are not going to tan the hide immediately it should be laid out flat to dry. However, it will shrink and wrinkle if it isn't stretched and tacked to a floor, wall, or sheet of plywood. After it has dried thoroughly, it can be removed and put away in a cool, dry place. It must be protected from dogs, cats, mice, and insects; on way to do this is to sprinkle it on both sides with powdered borax.

ADJUSTABLE SKIN-STRETCHING FRAME

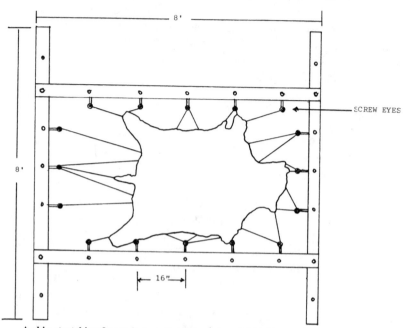

A skin-stretching frame is easy to make and useful in the tanning of most skins.

FLESHING AND DEGREASING

The first step in tanning is to soak the hide in soft water containing an ounce of borax for each gallon of water. Remember that the hide is to be tanned with the hair left on, and the greatest danger to such a skin in the tanning process is that it will be left in water too long so the hair starts to slip. Therefore, only soak the hide for four to six hours. If an agitator-type washing machine is available, place the hide in that and run the agitator so the solution will penetrate and soften the skin side of the hide quickly. About one hour in a washing machine with the water 99° F. will soften nearly any hide.

Usually a washing machine isn't available and the home tanner will be soaking his hide in a plastic garbage can and stirring it with a wooden paddle. In about two hours or as soon as it is flexible, the hide should be taken out of the water and hung up to drain for a few minutes. Then flop it hair side down on the fleshing beam and flesh off all the remaining bits of fat and meat. It is helpful at this stage to have a fleshing knife with teeth to scrape the hide so the thin membrane that separates the hide from the fat is removed; any sections of membrane left on the hide will cause it to pucker when it dries. If this should happen, the membrane must be scraped off later and the spot left untanned is finished with a spot paste tan.

After you are satisfied that the hide is well fleshed, it will have to be degreased. Fats and oils in a bearskin will almost certainly cause a disruption in the tanning process, so it is best to degrease a bearskin by immersing it in clear kerosene or white gasoline. Plunge and knead the skin in the bath for fifteen to twenty minutes. Then make sure the skin is completely immersed and let it soak overnight in the kerosene bath. When the degreasing is complete, squeeze all the degreaser you can get out of the skin.

Wash the bearskin in a detergent solution made by mixing two full tablespoons of Tide or Ivory soap to each gallon of water. Don't soak the skin in this solution, just wash it thoroughly. Then rinse the detergent out with lukewarm water, plunging and working the skin, and changing the water as often as necessary until no more soap bubbles come up.

After rinsing, dry the hair with a hair dryer, a vacuum cleaner, or warm sawdust rubbed into the hair. Let it set for ten minutes to absorb the moisture, and then hang it over a clothesline and beat it with a heavy switch to get the sawdust out. The flesh side of the hide should be kept damp so it will absorb the tanning solution; if it dries out hard and stiff, soften it by laying it hair side down and covering the flesh side with damp cloths. It will probably take eight hours or more for the hide to soften.

TANNING THE HIDE

A bearskin rug can be immersion tanned with chrome crystals or paste tanned with alum and gambier. Immersion tanning is the easiest, but if the hair has started to loosen, use the paste tan to set the hair again as well as provide a satisfactory tanning job.

Chrome Tanning Bearskin

Chrome tan a bearskin by first weighing the degreased hide, and then mixing eight ounces of salt and one gallon of water together for each pound of hide. When the salt is well dissolved, put the skin in the solution and let it soak for one half hour. While it is soaking, mix up the chrome solution by adding three ounces of chrome powder to one quart of 100° F. water for each pound of hide. Using this formula, a ten-pound skin will require eighty ounces of salt, thirty ounces of chrome, and 12½ gallons of water.

After one half hour, remove the skin from the salt solution and add half of the chrome-tanning solution. Stir it well and replace the skin in the container, stirring and turning the skin several times in the next twelve hours. Then remove the skin, add the rest of the chrome liquid, stir it well, and replace the skin. Thereafter stir it several times a day and closely watch the skin to see when the chrome has completely penetrated. This might take about three days, but as soon as it is done remove the skin and rinse the chrome solution from the skin in clear water.

Then neutralize the tanning liquid by immersing the skin in a solution made by dissolving ten ounces of sodium bicarbonate in ten gallons of water. Soak and plunge the skin in this liquid for about one hour. After the sodium bicarbonate bath, the skin must be rinsed in clean water to complete the tan.

Paste Tanning Bearskin

The alum gambier paste tan also starts after the skin has been degreased. Either lace it into a stretching frame or lay it out hair side down on a wooden floor or sheet of plywood, and tack it down very well so it doesn't wrinkle or shrink during the tanning process.

Tacking down a skin will proceed more aptly if a definite procedure is followed. Smooth the skin out as flat as possible; then tack the head skin down, and place a nail on either side rather than in the bare nose area. When the head is fastened to the board, go to the rump area and pull the skin so it is just taut, putting in several nails to hold it in place. Now go to either side, spread the skin on each side as far as it will go, and tack it down. This will spread the skin in a cross-shaped pattern. Work your way all around the skin, stretching and pulling so the slack and wrinkles are out of it. The leg and paw skins have to be spread open and nailed to keep them open. Use 6 or 8d nails placed about every six inches around the outer rim of the hide.

When the hide is stretched, mix up the combination tanning solution containing one pound of aluminum sulfate, one pound of salt, and three ounces of gambier or terra japonica. Dissolve the aluminum sulfate and salt together in warm water; then heat one quart of water to the boiling point and stir the gambier into the water. Add the aluminum sulfate and salt solution to the gambier and water, and pour the mixture into two gallons of clean, soft water. To make a paste, pour

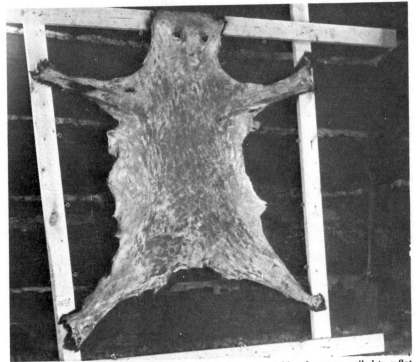

After the skin is fleshed very well, it is stretched on a stretching frame or nailed to a flat surface to keep it from shrinking.

part of the tanning solution in a pan and add wheat flour to make a thin paste. Mix additional paste as needed.

Use a spoon or dipper to apply the tanning solution to the skin side of the staked out bear hide. Be sure to cover it very well with a coating of at least ⅛ inch thick. Each day for two days in a row, scrape off the old solution and add a new layer to make a total of three layers of tanning solution added to the skin. The skin should be kept covered with plastic sheeting or cloths except when applying a new layer of tanning solution so it doesn't dry out.

After the third layer has set a day, test the skin to see if it is properly tanned by cutting off a thin sliver at the edge. It should be evenly colored throughout.

If the tanning looks like it is complete, remove the cloths from the skin and let it dry for about one day. When it is almost dry, scrub the flour paste off the skin with a scrub brush and warm water. Then demount the hide and immerse it in a borax water bath using one ounce of borax to the gallon of water. Let it soak in the borax solution for twenty minutes and then rinse the solution out by immersing the skin in clear water. Soak it for twenty minutes and then squeeze and wring out all the water that you can. Then place it on a fleshing beam and use the slicker to further remove excess moisture.

SOFTENING AND FINISHING THE FUR

While the bearskin is still damp, tack it out again on a smooth surface, flesh side up, and apply a thin coating of neat's-foot oil. However, if the skin tends to be oily and flexible, this step can be eliminated. When it is nearly dry the skin can be removed and placed on the fleshing beam, pulling bench, or staking tool and softened. Increased flexibility will make the hide flat which is an important consideration when making a bear rug. If some areas are humped, the skin should be shaved or sanded to make the area more flexible.

If the steps mentioned were correctly done, the skin is now tanned and ready to be made into a rug or a wall hanging. You can turn the skin over to a taxidermist for finishing or do it yourself. If you finish the skin yourself, the first step is to get it as flat as possible so it can be trimmed.

If the hide doesn't lie flat, relax it by sponging a carbolic acid solution of one gallon of water with 1½ tablespoons of carbolic acid on the flesh side. Sponge enough solution on the flesh to thoroughly dampen it, and then roll it up and let it set overnight. If it isn't completely relaxed the next morning, repeat the application and roll it up again for another night. When it is as limp as possible, tack it out on a flat surface pulling it as tight as you can get it. Tack it securely and leave it until it dries.

When it is dried, remove the skin from the stretching board, lay it hair side down, and trim the sides to make it symetrical. Do this by drawing a chalk line down the center of the back of the skin. Create a grid by drawing straight chalk lines six inches apart from this center line to the outside edge of the skin. Carefully measure these lines and trim the edges of the belly skin and the thin underarm skin so each side is even.

If the skin still humps up, cut wedges into the outside edges of the skin, draw the edges together, and sew them. Finally, "poison" the skin to keep insects and animals from chewing it by sponging a thick application of a borax and formaldehyde solution on the flesh side. Make the solution by mixing one gallon of water with four ounces of powdered borax and twenty-five drops of forty percent formaldehyde.

The tape on this bearskin indicates where the skin will be trimmed to make it symmetrical.

Bearskin rugs are often padded underneath with sponge rubber or blanket material, and this padding is covered with a tough, cloth underlining material.

HOW AND WHERE TO COLLECT BLACK BEAR IN THE U.S. AND CANADA

There's an old saying among hunters, "Go where the game lives," so the beginning bear hunter will probably have a better chance of collecting a bear if he hunts in the state or province where large bear

A completely tanned and trimmed bearskin rug.

populations exist. The top states are listed in order of the number of bears harvested, according to Department of Natural Resource figures.

Alaska	4000 per year mostly in southeast Alaska
Vancouver Island, British Columbia	4000 per year
Ontario	4000 per year
Washington	2500 per year
Quebec	numbers unknown, but substantial
Idaho	2000 per year
Montana	1850 per year
Maine	1000 per year
New York	750 per year
Colorado	700 per year
Minnesota	1269 high but 500 to 600 average per year
Wisconsin	1250 high but 500 to 600 average per year
Michigan	900 high but 400 to 600 average per year

Black bear populations are high at present all across North America, and in some places they are underharvested. If you would rather have an off-color bear, you would do well to hunt in the West where most of them are cinnamon colored. Black bears vary in color from nearly all black to cream colored, blond, red-brown, or chocolate, and an individual bear might change color in his lifetime. One coal black bear sow was seen with one brown cub, one albino cub, and one red-brown youngster.

8

Tanning Thin Domestic Animal Skins

There are many reasons why the home tanner will want to tan sheepskins, goatskins, calfskins, and pigskins. Calfskins can be made into garments and rugs; goatskins make nice garments; and sheepskins are useful for rugs, jackets, vests, mittens, bed pads, hats, and holsters.

TANNING SHEEPSKIN

Skinning the Sheep

First, let's examine sheepskin tanning. The sheep has to be skinned, and this is done by hanging it up by the hind legs with a gamble arrangement. Sheep seldom weight more than 100 pounds, so even holding one suspended on your own isn't a formidable task. To skin a sheep, use a sharp knife and part the wool so it doesn't contaminate the meat when you are removing it. Make a knife slit between the hind legs, down the belly, and all the way through the lower lip. Use the knife to circle the front legs at the knee, then make a slit up the inside of the front legs from the belly cut. Go to the hind legs and make a knife slit up the inside of each hind leg to the belly cut after making a circle cut around each hock.

Starting at the hocks, work the skin loose around the hind legs down to the belly cut, and then carefully work the skin loose around the hips, being careful not to let the wool brush the meat. Sheep are skinned very easily when they are warm, so after the hind legs are skinned out, the hide can be pulled down over the body without further knife cuts. Continue to pull it downward, skinning out the front legs as you go. Once past the front legs, the hide should pull easily down to the head where it must be cut loose from the ears, eyes, and lips. From a practical standpoint, the head skin can be cut off at the neck at this time since there is little area on it to be turned into leather. However, the industry method is to retain the head skin.

Salting the Hide

Usually the hide isn't fleshed at this point except to hand pull off any large chunks of fat or flesh. Lay the hide wool side down on a flat surface, and salt it down very well, using a pound of salt for each pound of hide. Pour a good quantity of salt along the center of the hide and then rub it into the skin, working outwards from the backbone until all the hide is well coated. Fold the hide once, roll it up, and let it stand with one end elevated so the liquid can run out. After thirty-six hours, unroll the hide, scrape the salt off, and resalt it. This time leave the hide for twenty-four hours, and then lay it out flat to dry. After it has dried it will keep for up to two years in a cool place.

Fleshing and Cleaning the Skin

When you are ready to use it, place the hide in a container of cool water containing a small amount of household bleach. Let it soak until it is soft, which will probably take about twelve hours. Then take it out, let it drain, place it wool side down on a fleshing beam or table, and scrape off all the flesh and fat and the tough, transparent membrane.

Fill a tub with warm (110 to 120° F.) water containing enough soap to create a good layer of soap suds. Immerse the skin in this and scrub out all the dirt and foreign matter. Rinse the skin very well, dump out the water, make a fresh batch of soap suds, and add ¼ cup of chlorine bleach. Return the skin to the water and let it soak, moving it around in the water. After fifteen minutes, take the skin from the soap suds, dump the soapy water out, and fill the tub with warm clean water.

Sheepskins flesh easily, and with practice it is only about a ten-minute job. Use a double-handled fleshing knife and don't press so hard that you rip the skin.

Rinse the skin in enough baths to remove all of the soap and then wring it out until it is just a little damp.

Tanning the Woolly Hide

Tawing Tan. Now the tawing solution can be applied to the flesh side. Mix ½ pound of alum, ¼ pound of saltpeter, 1½ pounds of bran moistened with warm water, and stir to a paste; then completely cover the flesh side of the skin with the solution. Fold the halves of the skin together with the flesh side in, roll it up, and set it in a cool place for one week. To finish the tan, unroll the hide, scrape off the bran, and rub it on a metal washboard or similar device until the skin is soft and supple.

Acid Pickle Tan. One of the easiest ways to tan a sheepskin utilizes a washing machine and an acid pickle tan process. Usually the sheep or lamb is kept for six weeks after shearing so the wool has grown

Nearly all sheepskins must be washed in warm water before they can be tanned. A strong solution such as Tide and Clorox bleach is added to the water to increase its cleaning ability. Two washings followed by a good rinse will clean almost any skin. A plastic garbage can with a cover is a fine container for washing and tanning sheepskins. A wooden paddle and a water pail are also needed.

back to the "shearling" stage and can be used for slippers and bed pads. Try to use pelts that are free from tick bites and shearing cuts, and be very careful not to nick the hide when skinning the animal. Flesh it very well, let the skin cool, and then sprinkle the skin side with a strong household detergent, and brush it in with a stiff brush.

Now wash the pelt in the washing machine with lukewarm water and detergent. Rinse and spin out the water using the spin cycle of the machine, and this should remove all the loose fat as well as the dirt and blood.

Using a plastic or wooden container, mix one gallon of water, one pound of pickling salt, and four ounces of unused automotive-type sulfuric acid together for each pound of skin. *Use extreme caution in handling sulfuric acid.* First dissolve the salt in the water, and then slowly pour the acid into the salt solution, stirring it very well.

Immerse the pelt and stir it gently. Then weight it down so it doesn't float on top of the liquid and let it soak, stirring it twice a day for at least five days.

Now remove the pelt from the tanning solution, and spin out the liquid in the spin cycle of your washing machine. Rinse the pelt twice

Nearly everything needed to acid tan a skin is shown in this picture. First weigh the skin, then add salt and sulfuric acid according to the formula.

in clear water and then spin out the rinse water. Now neutralize the skin by immersing it in a solution made by dissolving one ounce of borax in each gallon of water. Work the skin in the borax solution for one hour and then rinse and spin out the rinse water in the machine.

Lay the pelt wool side down on a 4- × -8-inch piece of ½-inch plywood and tack it out flat. Use long nails, and slide the skin up to the head of the nails so there is space between the wool and the plywood. Apply a thin coat of neat's-foot oil to the flesh side and let it soak for eight hours or until the oil has disappeared. While it is soaking, direct the air from a fan across the wool side of the pelt so it dries out as quickly as possible. Once the neat's-foot oil has soaked in, apply a thin coating of tanning oil on the flesh side.

After the tanning oil has soaked in enough so that white spots start to appear, remove the skin from the stretching frame and soften it by staking and stretching it or tumbling it in the electric clothes dryer. When it is completely dry, it can be sandpapered on the flesh side to make it smooth. Use a metal comb to comb out the wool, and if the wool seems fuzzy and dried out, rub hair dressing into it and brush it gently. Sheepskins tanned by this process cannot be washed in water; they are dry cleaned or cleaned with gasoline dampened sawdust.

Inspect the skin thoroughly several times during the tanning process to make sure everything is proceeding smoothly. The tanning solution will penetrate from both the wool side and the flesh side.

Glutaraldehyde Tan. Sheepskins can also be tanned with glutaraldehyde. Tanned this way, sheepskins are very useful because they can be used for articles of clothing that can be washed like cloth and are almost impervious to shrinkage under normal conditions. This substance also has the ability to keep leather from rotting from perspiration and is widely used in combat boots and fine hunting boots.

Start preparing the sheepskins by softening them in a solution of ½ cup of detergent soap for each five gallons of water. It should be washed repeatedly until the water stays clean when the hide is immersed. Continue rinsing the skin and changing the wash water and then drain the hide.

Before the skin completely dries out, put it on the fleshing beam and scrape off all the excess tissue right down to the under layer of skin, but be careful—sheepskin rips easily. Thoroughly rinse the fleshed hide in lukewarm water to remove all of the loose flesh and accumulated dirt from the wool.

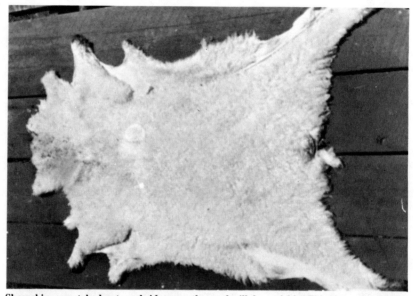

Sheepskins are staked out wool side up so the wool will dry quickly. This is necessary when soaking the skin to release it after acid tanning, or when "carding" it to remove burrs and sticks caught in the wool.

Before tanning, weigh the skin, and for each pound of hide dissolve ten ounces of noniodized salt in five quarts of lukewarm water (85 to 90° F.) in a clean, watertight, wooden or plastic barrel. A stainless steel or enameled container may be substituted but do not use galvanized iron or aluminum. Stir with a wooden paddle until the salt is dissolved; then add 2¼ ounces of twenty-five percent glutaraldehyde solution. Stir this in carefully to avoid splashing, and do not inhale the vapors because the chemical is very irritating.

When the glutaraldehyde is well mixed into the salt solution, carefully immerse the skin and slowly stir it with a wooden paddle for five minutes. Stir it for one minute each hour of the first day, and make sure the container is covered during the night and any other time it is not being stirred. At the end of the day, the skin and the wool will have turned a pale yellow.

On the second day, stir the hide for one minute each hour, keeping the barrel covered between stirring and during the night. On the third day, continue this for another six to eight hours, (a total of fifty-four to fifty-six hours), and then drain the barrel and rinse the skin in several changes of clear, lukewarm water.

Lay the wet skin over the beam to drain overnight. Make a fat-liquor emulsion by mixing one cup of neat's-foot oil with one cup of water for each twenty-five pounds of sheepskin. Add two ounces of household bleach for each pint of oil-water mixture, stir well, and divide the fat-liquor in two parts.

After it has drained, place the sheepskin on a flat surface and use a paint brush or your hand to apply a thin coat of the emulsion to the skin side of the hide, but be careful to keep it off the wool. Be sure to cover all of the skin; let it set for thirty minutes, and then apply another coat with the second portion. Cover the flesh side with a sheet of plastic to prevent drying and leave it overnight.

The next day, remove the plastic, turn the skin wool side up, and allow it to dry; while it is still damp, spread it out on a stretching frame, and nail or tie it taut but not overly tight. Let it dry to the damp stage, and then stake it until it is soft and flexible. The hide should be sanded with sandpaper to thin down any thick places. When tanned by this process, the sheepskin can be washed.

Tanning the Dehaired Sheepskin

Sometimes it is desirable to tan sheepskin with the wool removed—a product widely used as "buckskin." If the wool hasn't been sheared, it can be pulled off after the hide is treated with a dehairing solution. The wool is then cleaned and sold.

The first step is to clean the sheepskin if it is extremely dirty. If the wool is to be saved, lay the skin wool side down on the floor and spread the flesh side with a dehairing paste made by wetting 2½ pounds of caustic lime with enough water to make a paste. Spread this on the flesh side with a paddle, and leave the skin in a warm room until the wool pulls. Pull out the wool, set it aside, and flesh and tan the skin like buckskin. Commercial tanners use hydrated lime and sodium sulfide to loosen the hair roots; they then pluck the wool by machine.

If the sheepskin has been sheared or the wool is not to be saved, the hide is immersed in a dehairing solution made by adding 1½ pounds of lime to five gallons of water. Leave the hide in this solution until the wool slips easily which will usually take thirty-six to forty-eight hours. Scrape the wool and the upper layer of skin off as you would buckskin. Tan sheep leather with alum chrome tan or one of the synthetic tans.

TANNING GOATSKIN

Goatskins can be made into some highly regarded leather. Morocco leather, glacé kid, sueded kid, and true kidskins from young goats are used for shoes, gloves, and other garments. The home tanner will often find use for such leather since goatskins are economical and plentiful. Goatskin makes a very good substitute for deerskin or calfskin.

Kidskins will weight fourteen ounces when dried, a doe goatskin from 1½ to 2 pounds, and the skin from an adult male from three to five pounds. The best goatskins come from animals that range in pasture and are not supplementally fed. Goats that are fed heavily build up fat cells in the corium skin layer; this weakens the leather so much that it is practically useless for most purposes. When goats are kept inside, their sweat glands are so active that the skin is adversely affected.

The time of year greatly influences the quality of goatskins also. In summer, the hide is full of blood vessels and perishable nutrients, and is difficult to cure correctly. In winter, the excess blood and nutrients have been transferred into the hair, and the skin is white and capable of receiving a good tan.

Skinning the Goat

A goat should always be skinned when it is warm. If the carcass cools, the skin shrinks, and the ligaments which attach the skin to the body toughen and are hard to remove.

For skinning a goat, it is hard to beat the English method. Suspend the goat by the hind legs or lay it on its back, and make a shallow, careful cut up the exact center of the belly from between the teats to the center of the breast bone. Be sure not to cut too deeply and puncture the intestines. Now go back to the origin of the first cut, and make a cut up the inside of the hind legs past the hock joint. Use your fingers and a small wedge, not a knife, to loosen the skin around the belly and thighs.

Continue the hind leg cuts to the hoof, strip off the leg skin, and entirely remove it from the leg. Now go back to the belly and loosen the skin around the sex organs and anus and cut around these openings. Cut up the underside of the tail, and pull the tail out of the skin. Using your fingers and a wooden wedge, peel the skin from the flanks and back, loosening the skin up to the chest. Continue the belly cut up to the throat and work the skin free from the chest. Now skin up the inside of the front legs and peel this skin off. Next cut around the head, pull this skin off the neck, and the hide is free.

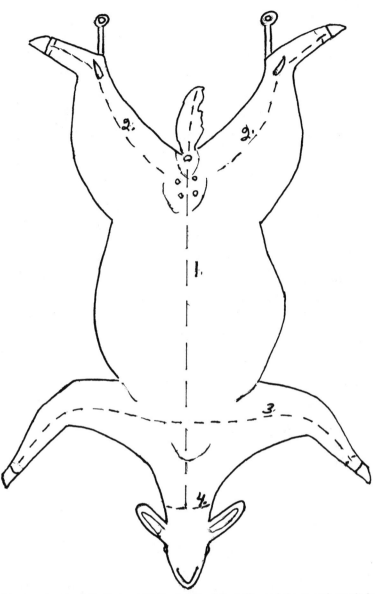

To skin a goat, extend the first cut (1) the length of the belly, and the second cut (2) from the belly up the insides of the hind legs. The third cut (3) is up the inside of the front legs to the hoofs, and (4) finally, you circle the head.

Fleshing the Skin

When the hide is free, it should be fleshed very well to remove all of the flesh, gristle, and membrane. Gaotskins are fairly difficult to flesh, and I have had the best luck using a long blade butcher knife kept as sharp as it normally is to cut bread and meat. When using a sharp knife, great care has to be used to avoid skin cuts. If the skin is to be stored it should be salted by covering the flesh side of the skin with one pound of salt to each pound of skin.

Degreasing the Skin

Properly prepared goatskins can be tanned by any of the conventional tanning formulas. If the skin is to be tanned with the hair on, it might have to be degreased to eliminate the high odor which some goats have. Degrease the goatskin by immersing it in a bath of white gasoline, kerosene, or alcohol for ten to fifteen minutes while working and scrubbing it. Don't soak, but scrub the skin in a detergent solution made by adding two tablespoons of strong detergent to each gallon of water. Be sure to rinse out the soap with clean water.

Dehairing the Hide

If the goatskin is to be made into leather, it must be dehaired. If it is necessary, relax the goatskin by soaking it in clear water until it is soft.

Then mix up a solution by combining 1½ pounds of lime with five gallons of water. Immerse the skin and let it soak, moving it around at least once a day. In three to ten days the hair will loosen, and it can be scraped off with the fleshing knife.

After dehairing, goatskins are "bated." First rinse out the lime by soaking the skin for one hour in three changes of water. Then add ½ pint of vinegar to each five gallons of water and soak the skin overnight to neutralize all of the lime solution. Again, rinse the skin in three changes of clean water, moving it around and squeezing it to remove all lime residue.

Tanning the Hide

After the rinse, the skin can be tanned by the following process, either with the hair on or off. Immerse the skin for six hours in a pickling solution made by combining four gallons of cold, soft water,

½ ounce of borax, ½ pint of salt, and four ounces of automotive-type sulfuric acid. Let the skin soak for six hours. Next mix two gallons of cold, soft water, two pints of salt, and four ounces of pulverized oxalic acid. Immerse the skin and let it soak, moving it around at least once a day. A thin kidskin will be thoroughly tanned in forty-eight hours, a thicker buck goatskin might take up to five days. Close inspection of the skin will indicate when the tan has completely penetrated.

When the tan is done, rinse the hide thoroughly in several changes of clean water and hang it to dry. If the goatskin is well pulled while it is drying, it will soften. If it dries before softening, cover it with damp cloths, let it set until the skin is relaxed, and then pull it again until it is soft. Goatskins will probably not have to be fat-liquored to soften them.

TANNING CALFSKIN

Calfskins are often tanned since they yield high quality leather and attractive robes. Moreover, they are considerably easier to handle than cow or bull hides. Calfhides are usually available from slaughterhouses or farmers who do their own butchering. Grade calves often have spotted and dappled hides which yield attractive rugs and vests. Use the same methods for tanning calfhides as for tanning cowhides.

TANNING PIGSKIN

Home tanners may sooner or later want to try tanning a pigskin, and this is well within the capabilities of the amateur tanner. Pigskin is used for a variety of leather projects such as gloves, mittens, shoe uppers, and handbags. When vegetable or chrome tanned, pigskin is very durable; well softened, it can be used for vests and other garments.

Skinning the Pig

First hang the pig up and skin it instead of scalding the skin first so the hair will come off as is customary. Pigs are skinned in the traditional way by first making a shallow cut down the exact center of the belly from the base of the lower jaw to the rectum. Try not to cut through the fat. Make a cut up the center of the inside of the front legs to the first joint. Circle the joint with the knife and strip the hide off of the front legs. It will be necessary to use the knife to cut the skin loose. Leaving as much fat on the carcass as possible will save considerable work in fleshing the skin later. When the front leg skin has

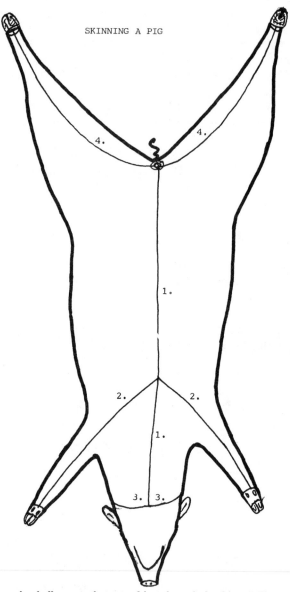

SKINNING A PIG

To skin a pig, make shallow cuts that extend just through the skin. (1) First slice down the belly from the lower jaw to the rectum, (2) and then up the front legs to the joint. (3) Circle cut around the head and finish by cutting up the inside of each hind leg and around the joint.

been loosened, go to the origin of the cut at the lower jaw and make a circle cut all around the base of the head. Use the knife to loosen this skin and start peeling it off, pulling and shaving the fat off the inside of the skin as you go.

When you get to the center of the pig's body with the loosened skin, make slits down the inside of each hind leg to the hock and skin the hind legs out. Make a circle cut around the anus and sex organs and continue to pull and cut the skin downward until it comes off the hips.

Fleshing the Skin

If care was used in removing the skin, there should only be a minimum of fleshing to be done. However, pigskin has a tough membrane covering the inside of the skin, as do other mammal skins, and it must be removed. Use a toothed scraper to break this up, if one is available. If desired, the tissue can be softened and fleshing made easier by soaking the skin overnight in a solution made by combining one ounce or more of powdered borax with one gallon of water. This will make the skin somewhat easier to flesh.

After fleshing the pigskin should be degreased by immersing the skin in kerosene for twelve hours or overnight. Remove the skin from the kerosene bath and wash it in warm water and detergent followed by rinses in two changes of clean water. Use ½ cup strong household detergent for each gallon of 110 to 120° F. water. It can also be scrubbed with warm sawdust or kitty litter to remove the kerosene.

Dehairing the Hide

To dehair the hide, mix up a solution of three pounds of lime to ten gallons of water. Soak the skin overnight, and the next morning it will probably be easy to scrape the bristle or hair off the hide; if not, return the skin to the solution for an additional day. Scrape the flesh side of the pigskin again and it is ready to pickle.

Tanning the Skin

Using a plastic, glass, or wooden container, pickle the pigskin before chrome tanning to aid in the complete penetration of the tanning solution. Weigh the skin, and for every pound of skin mix one pound of salt and four ounces of thirty-three percent sulfuric acid in one gallon of soft water. Immerse the skin and let it soak for twenty-four hours, or until the entire skin has attained an even color and plumpness. Then remove the skin from the pickle and rinse it.

Although some tanners do not neutralize the skin between the pickle and the chrome bath, most projects seem to yield better results if they are neutralized. To neutralize the skin, immerse it in a bath made by dissolving one ounce of bicarbonate of soda in each gallon of water. Soak the skin for two hours, stirring it occasionally, then rinse it in two changes of water.

Now mix eight ounces of salt and one gallon of water together for each pound of skin, and immerse the skin, letting it soak for half an hour. While it is soaking, mix one quart of warm water and three ounces of chrome powder together for each pound of skin.

In half an hour, remove the skin from the salt solution, pour half the chrome liquid into the salt, stir it well, and return the skin to the solution. Plunge it up and down a few times and let it soak for twelve hours, stirring it at least twice during this time. In twelve hours or more, remove the skin, pour the rest of the chrome solution into the container, stir it well, and return the skin to the bath. Let it soak until the blue tanning color has completely penetrated the skin. Remove the skin and rinse it very well to remove all excess tanning solution. Neutralize the mixture with a bicarbonate of soda bath as before.

Softening and Finishing the Pigskin

When this process is complete, the pigskin will be tanned, but it will be a light blue color and it will probably be somewhat stiffer than is desirable. It can be dyed with hemlock bark, oak bark, fabric dyes, or leather dyes. Oiling it with neat's-foot oil will also change the color. See chapter 13 for dyeing methods.

Pigskins are softened like other skins. Before the skin dries completely, tumble it in a clothes dryer or work it over a stake. If the skin is thick, it should be shaved or sanded to reduce the thickness and aid in softening it. A good quality tanning oil will also help considerably in softening it.

9

Tanning Thick Domestic Hides For Rugs, Robes, or Leather

Domestic horse and cow hides have traditionally been turned into useful, beautiful, and long-lived items for home and dress. They can be successfully tanned by many different methods, some of which are simple and fast. A great advantage of working with a domestic skin is it is much easier to acquire than a bear or moose hide; most farms and slaughterhouses have hides that they sell by the pound. A typical hide might cost from ten to twenty dollars.

To avoid the possibility of disease, don't work with a hide from an animal that has died of natural causes. Be sure to examine the hide for skinning cuts since some hides would be more trouble to sew up again than it would be worth. Also, avoid hides that are excessively caked with dirt and manure.

PREPARING TO TAN A DOMESTIC HIDE

Tanning Materials

Once the hide is obtained, the next step is to find a large container if you don't have one. A wooden fifty-gallon barrel is ideal if available;

Horse hide makes fine heavy leather, or it can be tanned with hair on for rugs or robes.

some possible sources of supply are the discards from wineries, distilleries, and vegetable-processing centers. If you can't get a wooden barrel, a large, sturdy, plastic garbage can will also fit the bill. If neither is available, you can use a metal barrel by lining it with three heavy-duty plastic bags placed inside of each other.

Besides the barrel, you will need about fifty pounds of salt, a large fleshing knife, and a large fleshing beam or a table that can be used for a fleshing beam. Try to position the barrel under overhead beams so that some sort of hoist arrangement can be used for lifting the skin and suspending it to drain or inspect.

After acquiring your hide and materials, prepare the hide by laying it out on a flat surface, pulling it into a rectangular shape, and nailing it down. Then trim away the ends of the legs, the head skin, and any irregular parts that extend beyond the main section of the hide. When you finish, the skin should resemble a blanket. If it is very heavy, split it down the center along the backbone and sew it back together after you finish tanning. Trim away any large amounts of flesh and fat from the hide, although it will also be well fleshed later.

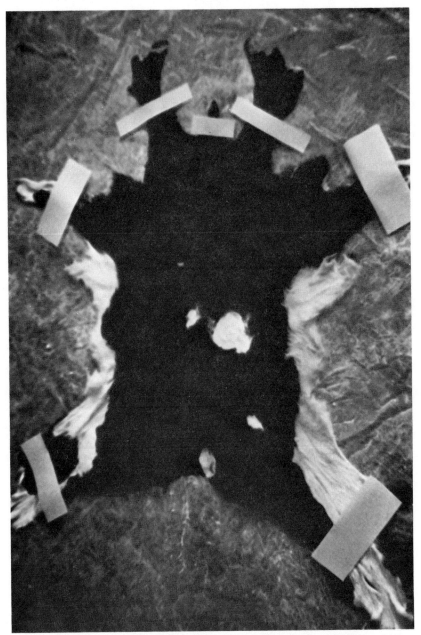
Most cattle hides are trimmed as shown before they are tanned. If the skin is laced into a stretching frame, fewer laces are needed to stretch the hide after it is trimmed.

Salting the Skin

The next step is to salt the hide well. Salt opens the pores of the hide so that later tanning operations will be more effective. If the hide is dirty or stiff, it can be salted and soaked at the same time. Do this by filling the barrel with a saturated salt solution that contains all the salt that the water will absorb. Mix it up a little at a time in a five- or ten-gallon container and add it to the tanning container. If the hide is extremely thick, it can be shaved or scored by making shallow knife cuts every inch over the thickest part (the back and neck) to insure absorption of the salt solution.

After the hide is left in the salt brine overnight or about twelve hours, the dirt and manure in the hide will have softened so they can be removed. Pull the hide out of the salt solution and dump out the salt brine. Salt of course is not poisonous, and if it is dumped in the woods, deer, rabbits, and porcupines will enjoy cleaning up whatever is left over. Refill the barrel with clean water and rinse the hide up and down in it several times to wash out as much dirt as possible. One expedient way to remove stubborn dirt is to flop the strips of skin hair side up on a fleshing beam and scrub them with a stiff brush or even push the dirt out with the back of a fleshing knife. Before the tanning starts the hide must be very clean.

If a hide is to be dry salted, you must treat the skin as soon as the body heat has left the animal. Use one pound of salt for each pound of hide, pouring the salt along the center of the backbone and spreading it out on each side until it covers all of the skin. Fold it in half and then roll it up and set it aside with one end higher than the other so the moisture can drain out. In two days unroll it and scrape off the old salt; resalt it again using one pound of salt for each pound of hide. Good results can also be obtained from stretching the hide on a stretching frame, salting it heavily, and then inclining one end so the moisture can run off. If salt is rubbed into the hide three times on alternate days the hide will salt dry and it will keep almost indefinitely if protected from predators, insects, and weather.

Fleshing and Softening the Skin

When the time comes to start tanning, find two sturdy sticks that will fit crossways in the barrel. Tie short lengths of rope to each of the sticks, drape the sides of the skins over the sticks, and lower them into the barrel. Then fill the barrel with fresh, clean water and soak the skins for two to three hours, stirring them several times. When they

The home tanner should salt a thick hide as soon as the body heat leaves the skin since it can start to deteriorate very fast. One way to do it is to pour salt down the center of the hide and spread it out to each side. Use a pound of salt for each pound of hide and rub it in very well.

are softened, remove them from the barrel, lay them out on the fleshing beam, and scrape off all the flesh and fat that you can remove at this time. Then work over the entire flesh side of the skin with the back of the knife; push extremely hard to remove the liquid fat and stretch the skin fibers. Wash the sides thoroughly with clean, cool water.

Refill the barrel by adding one ounce of borax to each gallon of water and return the hide to the bath. Let it soak for about one hour for a green skin or forty-eight hours for a dry-salted skin. Remove and drain the skin, lay it hair side down on the fleshing beam, and scrape off all the remaining fat and flesh. It should be made soft and pliable by scraping at this time. Rinse in clean water as the last step.

TANNING RUGS AND ROBES

A large cow or horse hide makes a very beautiful rug for laying over the back of a sofa or decorating a wooden floor. It imparts a warm rustic look that is not only distinctive but original because no two hides are ever exactly alike. When you select the hide, look for one that has a distinctive pattern (such as white marking on a brown hide) since the

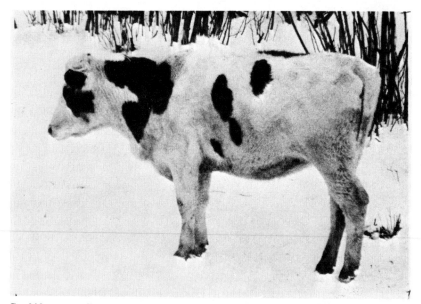

Cowhides are easily obtained from slaughterhouses and farmers. They can be made into virtually anything that leather is used for.

pattern will make an interesting contrast to the floor or furniture. A hide for a robe should measure about sixty by seventy-two inches.

If it is made soft and flexible enough, it is also useful as a bed comforter on frigid nights because no cold can penetrate the thick hide and hair of one of these robes. If you enjoy sleigh rides or other outdoor activities where you do not move enough to keep warm then the horsehide robe will protect you from the elements just as it did our ancestors. Skin robes are extremely long lived and many have been kept for seventy-five years or more, especially when they were protected from predation and treated once a year with a preservative.

Paste Tanning the Hide

For tanning the hides with the hair on, it's hard to beat the potash-alum-salt solution. Although aluminum sulfate is the tanning chemical, if salt is not used with it the skin will dry out hard and stiff and can't be softened. The fibers remain soft when salt is used because salt counteracts the effect of the sulfuric acid in the potash-alum mixture. The potash tan can be used either as an immersion tan or applied as a paste.

Good results can be obtained from tanning a robe with the paste method because the danger of the bacteria in water attacking the hair and causing it to slip is eliminated.

Stretch the skin out on a flat surface and tack it down after it has been properly fleshed and partially dried. Before it dries completely, mix up 1½ gallons of water, one pound of ammonia alum or potash alum, four ounces of washing soda, and eight ounces of salt. Thicken the mixture with bran or wheat flour to a paste and apply a good, thick layer to the flesh side of the skin. If one batch won't cover it, it might be necessary to mix up a second batch. Cover it with a sheet of plastic or a layer of newspaper so it doesn't dry too fast and let it stand this way for two days. Scrape off this layer and reapply another; repeat this in two more days, and this time don't cover it, but let it stand until the paste has dried. Check for penetration of the tanning liquid according to the previously mentioned test for tanning.

Immersion Tanning the Hide

The oxalic acid method of tanning by immersion has also been used successfully for robe skins. First prepare a pretanning soak: Add twenty-three gallons of soft, clean, cool water to the barrel and pour another gallon of warm water in a separate wood, glass, or plastic container. Add three pints of soft soap, three ounces of borax, and 4½ ounces of sulfuric acid to this gallon of warm water.

Add the solution to the water in the barrel and put the hide in, leaving it overnight or until it is soft and flexible. It should be stirred frequently. When the hide is soft, remove it from the barrel, let it drain, and then flesh it very well, removing all the flesh, fat, and skin membrane. Dump out the solution in the barrel, being careful to dispose of it where it will not contaminate a well or running water. Refill the barrel with clean water, rinse the hide, and work it over again with the fleshing knife to get rid of the dirty water and any clinging bits of flesh and fat.

The tanning can commence after this step if the hide is soft and porous. If not, continue to work it on the beam until it is. Then mix up two ounces of oxalic acid and one pound of salt to each gallon of water. It will require about twenty gallons of solution to tan a large hide. Add water until it covers the skin so it can be completely immersed.

Soak the skin in the oxalic acid solution for at least two days, stirring it at least twice a day. Check the skin for being completely tanned by slicing a section off the edge of the skin. It should show the white color clear through. Watch the hide carefully and remove it as soon as it is tanned because if it is immersed too long the hair might start to loosen.

A tanned cowhide robe which still needs some trimming before it is used.

After the tanning is complete, remove it from the barrel, dump out the oxalic acid solution in a safe place, rinse out the barrel, and refill it, adding one ounce of borax to each gallon of water. Soak the hide for about two hours, remove, wring it out as much as possible, and then dump out the borax solution and rinse the hide in several changes of clean water. Before it dries, stretch it out on a stretching frame and pull it taut. Rub neat's-foot oil or dubbin into the flesh side of the hide and stake it to whatever degree of softness is desired.

TANNING HEAVY LEATHER

Any hobby tanner is going to want to tan some of his own heavy leather sooner or later since it can be used as shoe soles, belting, harness leather, dog collars, gun cases, knife sheaths, luggage, etc. To make leather proceed as follows: Cool, salt, and flesh the skin according to the directions given for the robe tanning. Be sure to clean the hide very well and to flesh it smooth and soft before the dehairing procedure.

Dehairing the Hide

Prepare a dehairing bath made of ten pounds of fresh hydrated lime dissolved very well in five gallons of water. Once all the lumps of lime are worked out, add enough clear water to fill the barrel and stir it again. Now take the sides of hide and hang them over the stick supports previously described and lower them into the lime water solution. Make sure they are covered by the lime water. The hide will have to soak for several days but it should be moved around every day and the solution should be kept stirred up.

It might require from ten days to two weeks for the hair to be correctly loosened. Long before this time it will be loose enough to be pulled out, but when it is ready it can be rubbed off by hand.

When the hair is loose, remove the hide and hang it over a beam to drain. Then flop it on the fleshing beam and use the fleshing knife to scrape off all the hair and the black layer of hair roots. If some tight patches are encountered, return it to the barrel and soak it some more.

When you have the hair scraped off, the hide can be fleshed again using a sharp knife. The thickest places can be shaved until the hide is uniform while you are removing the fat and flesh.

Deliming the Skin

The lime must be removed from the skins by rinsing them several times in clear water, changing the water at least four times, and working the skin around in the water with a paddle or by hand. Then soak the skin in clear water for five to six hours. Dump this water off, refill the barrel with clear water, and stir in five ounces of pure lactic acid or five pints of vinegar to the barrel. Soak the sides for twenty-four hours in the acid, then remove them, dump off the water, and refill it with clean, clear water and soak overnight. The sides are now ready to be tanned.

Bark Tanning Heavy Leather

Heavy leather can be vegetable or chrome tanned, but many people feel that vegetable tanning is better since the hide is less stretchy and probably will last longer. It does require alot more time though, especially if it is done the traditional way with layers of bark.

Either oak or hemlock bark can be used for steeping to produce a tanning solution. If equipment is available to grind it into powder, the time will be shortened considerably, but I have made an excellent tanning solution by soaking bark that was just cut up with an axe and it required very little work. The way I did this was to peel off the bark from a one foot diameter hemlock log, and chop the bark up into pieces about the size of a coat button with the hatchet.

Hemlock bark can be chopped up for use in tanning. The small pieces of bark require about two weeks of steeping before the tannin is all leached out.

I shortened the effort required for picking up the small pieces by chopping them up over a large sheet of plastic. At intervals I picked the plastic up with the bark held inside it and dumped them into a plastic garbage can that I use for tanning.

When I had the barrel nearly full of bark I poured enough rainwater in the barrel to completely cover the bark. Then I set the barrel in one corner of the room that I use for an office and let it set for six weeks, adding about three gallons of fresh bark in three weeks and enough water to keep it up to the top. At intervals throughout the session I checked the color of the liquid to see if the bark was giving up its tannic acid into the water, and indeed it was. In four weeks the liquid was very dark, and when after six weeks it didn't get any darker, I knew it was ready to use.

Vegetable tanning thick hides is an expedient way to handle them because the finished leather is so beautifully toned with a warm brown finish. Only vegetable-tanned leathers for instance, can be successfully tooled. They can be dampened and molded or stretched and will retain their shape when dry. They are the easiest to work with, they take dye well, and they can be finished to be as waterproof as any leather. What's more, vegetable tanning doesn't take any particular skills since little if any mixing of substances is required. About all the tanner has to do is to immerse the skin for the required time.

When I was ready to tan the skin it was summer, so I packed the barrel of tanning solution out to the garage that I use for a tanning workshop and placed the sides of skin that had been dehaired and fleshed properly in the tanning barrel. I wanted a tanning solution that would be about one percent tannin to start with, and so I poured five gallons of my tanning solution in the barrel, two quarts of vinegar, and rainwater until the mix covered the skin. I soaked the leather in this solution for ten days, and then each four days after that I took out five gallons of liquid and added five gallons more of the tanning mixture. I also stirred up the hide each day. In twenty-one days I sliced a section of the skin and the brown tannin color had nearly penetrated it completely.

Actually this test only indicated that the tanning process was proceeding correctly; if I had boiled a piece of skin at this stage it probably would have indicated that the tanning was not complete. My next step was to remove the sides and set them aside while I used a piece of screening to strain the bark out of the barrel. I retained the liquid since it was high in tannin content, and then I cut up a bushel of fresh bark, added it to the barrel, and replaced the skin. This time I left the sides in the barrel for three months, stirring them from time to time and replacing the water that had evaporated.

At the end of this time the leather was correctly tanned as proved by the tanning test. Although this process took time, it required no dangerous chemicals, it was not complicated, and it cost nothing. Moreover, it is impossible to overtan or otherwise ruin a skin by bark tanning it.

After the bark tanning was completed, I took the skin out of the tannin solution and rinsed it overnight in clear water to remove the brown tannin liquid. Then I removed the leather from the water and hung it up to drain. Next I laid it over the beam and scrubbed the grain side with plenty of water and a stiff brush. Then I slicked out both sides with the slicker, paying particular attention to the grain side which must be slicked in all four directions.

While the skin sides are still damp, go over them with a liberal coating of neat's-foot oil or cod-liver oil. Hang the sides up and let them dry slowly, then take them down and roll them up in a wet sack or burlap. When uniformly damp and limber, apply a thick coating of warm dubbin to the grain side of the hide, hang them up again, and leave them until uniformly dry. Take them down, and work them over with the slicker very well to remove the excess dubbin. Now apply a thin coat of warm dubbin on both the grain and flesh sides and hang them up to dry again. Finally take them down and work them over with the slicker again; if the surface is oily, rub them all over with sawdust.

Chrome Tanning Heavy Leather

Often heavy leather is chrome tanned either as a complete tan or as a prelude to vegetable tanning. Leather tanned in both ways is superior to leather tanned by one method only. Start chrome tanning by dehairing and fleshing the hide as previously outlined.

Chrome-tanned leather should be pickled before the chrome is applied. Pickle the hide by first squeezing the water out of it as much as possible, then weigh it and mix up a pickle bath by combining sixteen ounces of salt, four ounces of automotive (33⅓ percent) sulfuric acid, and one gallon of soft water together for each pound of hide. Thus a twenty-pound skin will require twenty pounds of salt, five pints of sulfuric acid, and twenty gallons of water. Mix the solution very well and immerse the skin in the pickle bath. Let it soak for twenty-four hours, stirring it very well.

In twenty-four hours remove the skin and rinse it in at least three changes of water, plunging and squeezing the skin to get out the acid.

Be sure to use rubber gloves and eye protection when working with sulfuric acid. This pickle bath can be reused for other skins, but after it is used twice it should be recharged by adding four pounds of salt and two pints of sulfuric acid. If you dump it out, be sure to dispose of it where it won't contaminate the drinking water of people or animals.

After the pickle bath is rinsed from the skin, mix a chrome bath of eight ounces of salt and one gallon of water for each pound of skin. This will require ten pounds of salt and twenty gallons of water for a twenty-pound skin. Put the skin in this saltwater and let it soak for one half hour. While it is soaking, mix three ounces of chrome crystals and one quart of 100° to 120° F. water together for each pound of skin. A twenty-pound skin will require five gallons of water and 3¾ pounds of chrome crystals.

Remove the skin, pour half the chrome solution in the saltwater, and stir it well. Then reimmerse the skin and let it soak for twelve hours, stirring it frequently. After twelve hours remove the skin, pour the remaining half of the chrome solution in the tanning container, and replace the skin. This time let it soak for five days stirring it frequently. After this time the skin should be colored completely through with the blue-green chrome color and it should pass the boiling test for tanning. If it doesn't, let it soak for another three days and test it again. No harm will come to the skin from being in the tanning solution past the stage when the tanning is complete.

After the skin is well tanned it has to be neutralized in a bath of one ounce of bicarbonate of soda to each gallon of water. Rinse the skin in clear water, put it in a clean container and add the neutralizing solution. Soak the skin for two hours, rinse it very well in clear water, and it is ready to oil and soften.

After rinsing, the heavy leather is coated on both sides with a liberal dressing of neat's-foot oil. After the oil is allowed to penetrate, the leather is slicked out with a slicker. Do this by stretching the hides out flat and then slicking from the center out. This action should push out the water and excess oil and smooth the outer surface of the leather. Heavy leather is not staked to soften it.

Oil Tanning Heavy Leather

A very fast way to prepare a heavy skin for use is to first soak, flesh, and dehair it according to the procedures already outlined. Neutralize the lime solution by soaking the dehaired hides for twenty-four hours in water in which 2½ ounces of lactic acid or 2½ pints of vinegar had been added to each twenty gallons of water. After this acid bath the hides should be soaked overnight in clear water to remove the acid.

Now stretch the hides on a frame either nailing them or sewing them to a rectangular frame large enough to stretch the hide very well. Let it dry to the damp stage and then rub a liberal coating of sulfonated neat's-foot oil, cod-liver oil, or a combination of the two into the leather. Warm the oil so it will penetrate better, and rub it in so it will not run off the hide. For a heavy skin at least four coats will be needed, each coat to be applied to alternate sides of the skin. It will usually require at least four to eight hours for the oil to soak into the leather. If the leather gets so hard that oil will not penetrate it, it can be softened by sprinkling it with warm water or covering it with damp cloths. When it is soft, apply another coat of oil.

Leather that is oil tanned like this is really not tanned at all: it is rawhide that has been well oiled. However, it has many of the qualities of tanned leather since it won't decay and it is waterproof. It can be made as soft as desired by staking it, but usually leather of this type is used for soles or gun cases or harnesses which don't require the leather to be soft. It has to be oiled from time to time during use to keep it from drying out.

If leather is to be dyed, this must be done before oil or grease is applied. If greased leather is to be dyed it must be degreased first by immersing it in white gasoline or naptha, and then regreased or fat-liquored to soften it. If you use the skin for sole leather it can be heavily oiled after it has been attached to the shoe by setting the shoes with the soles immersed in a pan of liquid dubbin or commercial water-proofing. Leave them in this mixture for twenty-four hours with the dubbin kept warm enough to be liquid but cool enough so it won't burn your hands.

10

Tanning Reptile, Fish, and Bird Skins

TANNING ALLIGATOR SKIN

Alligator populations have increased in some southern states until they are legal game again after being on the protected list for decades. The belly skin of the 'gator is a valuable product that can be made into top quality leather for shoes, handbags, gun cases, and belts.

The alligator is a reptile, and it looks like a lizard except the body and tail are much thicker. They have huge jaws with sharp teeth, and their eyes are placed high on their heads so they can see without rising above the water. They have short, thick legs that they use for walking; but when they swim, they hold their legs against their body and move their tails from side to side for propulsion.

A full grown bull alligator is a formidable beast, attaining a length of ten feet or more and a weight of 450 to 550 pounds. The females are smaller, but they also sometimes get to ten feet. Most alligators are much smaller though and probably average about six feet. Alligators live fifty to sixty years.

Most 'gators are trapped by setting a large fishhook in a piece of

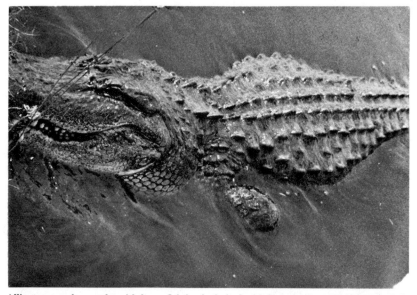

Alligators can be caught with large fish hooks baited with long-dead meat. Although their skin is very valuable after it is tanned, the back skin is too rough and thick to have much value.

meat. The hook is tied to a stout line and the line is tied to a tree on the bank. Sometime during the night the 'gator comes and swallows the hook, and he is caught.

Another way of getting 'gators is to cruise through the swamps and bayous after dark with a sturdy boat, a good light, and a deer rifle. When a 'gator's big red eyes are spotted he is shot with the rifle and then pulled aboard. One man was reputed to have shot 80 'gators in one night back in the early 1930s. Another got 4,000 'gators in one season. This large game bag probably contributed to the decline of the 'gator and for years he was listed as an endangered species. Now however, the season is open in Louisiana and a considerable number are harvested every year without hurting the breeding population.

Skinning an Alligator

An alligator should be skinned as soon as possible after he is captured. They skin easily for such a large animal, and an experienced skinner can remove the hide from a large alligator in a few minutes.

There are two methods of skinning an alligator; the Louisiana method leaves the back plate on the carcass, but this plate is so thick and tough that it is impossible to tan and soften it. Knife cuts are made from front to back along each side of the back plate and extend down along the outside of the legs to the wrists which are circle cut with the knife to loosen the leg skin. The hide is pulled off as much as possible and the knife is used only for loosening the skin around the legs.

When the back skin is to be saved, roll the animal on its back and make a knife cut along the center line of the belly from the tail to the underside of the jaw. The legs are skinned out by making a cut around

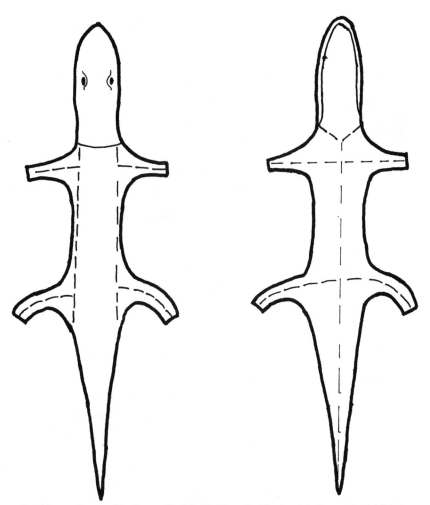

Louisiana alligator skinning method (left); "horn" alligator skinning method (right).

the wrist and a slit up the inside of the legs to the belly cut. The skin is stripped off by pulling, and the knife is used only when it is needed. Be extremely careful to avoid knife cuts because they greatly detract from the value of the skin.

Salting the Hide

Alligator hides putrefy easily, and they should be salted immediately after the skin is removed. Do this by rubbing fine salt into the flesh side, taking care to get the salt into all of the folds of the skin. Then fold the skin in half and roll it up. After two days the hide should be salted again, rolled up, and packed away in a barrel or bag, being careful to use enough salt to preserve it.

Fleshing the Hide

Alligator hides can be tanned using almost the same methods used for mammal skins. A dried hide should be soaked in clear water for two to four days until it is flexible and then it should be fleshed to remove all extraneous fat and flesh. Next put the hide in a bath made by dissolving three pounds of caustic lime in ten gallons of water to loosen the scales. The hide may have to soak in the lime bath for one to two weeks before the scales are loosened. When they will scrape off easily, they are removed with the back of the fleshing knife just like hair is removed from a mammal skin. When you finish scraping off the scales, beam the hide on both sides to clean and stretch it and to scrape away the excess protein.

Tanning the Hide

The chrome tan process works well for alligator hides. Wash the descaled hide well and then soak it for two hours in a solution made by dissolving 1½ ounces of boric acid crystals in one gallon of warm, soft water. This is important to neutralize any traces of lime left in the skin which would adversely affect the tanning process. Wash it again in clear water when it is removed from the lime, and then it is ready for the tanning liquid.

Make the chrome tanning liquid by dissolving three ounces of chrome alum and eight ounces of salt in a gallon of water for each pound of skin. Once all of the crystals are dissolved, place the skin in this solution and allow it to soak for four to five days, moving it around nearly every day. When the skin is tanned, the color of the chrome solution will have penetrated the skin completely.

The next step is to fix the chrome solution in the skin; this is done by adding one ounce of sodium carbonate in a half pint of warm water to the solution for each gallon of tanning fluid. Keep the skin in this solution for another week at least, moving the skin around each day.

Then remove the skin, drain it, and soak it overnight in a solution consisting of one part sulfonated neat's-foot oil to three parts of water. Remove and drain the skin the next day; then tack it on a frame to dry. When it is almost dry, remove the skin and work it over the breaking beam until it is soft and flexible. If the hide dries hard, it will have to be softened by rolling it in a damp cloth until it is flexible again.

TANNING FISH SKINS

Many fish have skin thick enough to be tanned into useful leather. Large northern pike, black bass, walleyes, and sturgeon have thick, useful hides that can be used for making pouches, bags, fishing lures, and coverings for rod handles.

Skinning the Fish

Use scissors to skin the fish, making a slit along the backbone from the tail to the head. Then cut downward on each side of the body just behind the head and along both sides of the body at the tail. Grasp the fold of skin at the back and cut and pull upwards, using a knife to trim the flesh from the skin as cleanly as possible. The fins can be left on the skin by cutting them off at the base as you skin out the fish.

Salting and Fleshing the Skin

Fish skins keep very well as rawhide, but they must be treated with borax or salt. Once the skin is removed, carefully flesh it with a sharp knife, and then rub fine salt into all the pores and folds of the skin to help dry it. It can also be immersed in a saturated salt brine to preserve the skin.

The rawhide skins are stretched on a board and left to dry. In the dried state they will keep almost indefinitely if protected from predators and moisture.

When the salted skin is to be tanned, soak it for an hour or two in clear water. Flesh the skin if necessary, taking care not to cut or rip it with the fleshing knife

Northern pike are plentiful, widely distributed, and always hungry. Their skin yields a fine leather after it is chrome tanned.

Descaling the Skin

Fish skins with scales must be descaled before they are tanned. Immerse the skin in a solution made by dissolving three ounces of caustic lime in one gallon of soft water. In one to five days time the scales will become very loose and they can be easily scraped off.

Next, rinse the skin in clear water and neutralize it by soaking it for two hours in a bath made by dissolving 1½ tablespoons of carbolic acid crystals in one gallon of water.

Tanning the Skin

Fish skins can be tanned by any of the chemical processes used for tanning fur skins. The alum and carbolic acid method is as good as any. First, flesh the hide very well. Meanwhile, dissolve ½ pound of salt, ¼ pound of alum, and ½ ounce of carbolic acid crystals in one gallon of water. Heat the water to between 120 and 130° F. and stir until all of the crystals are dissolved, allowing it to cool before proceeding.

Sturgeon skin is thick and rough. After being tanned it can be used for wall trophies, covering furniture, making containers, or even sandpaper.

Immerse the fish skin in the tanning solution and let it soak, stirring it now and then, until the skin is tanned completely through. This will take up to seven days.

When it is thoroughly tanned, remove it from the solution and immerse it for about two hours in a bath made by combining one ounce of bicarbonate of soda with one gallon of water. Then take it out, drain it, and rinse it off in clear water.

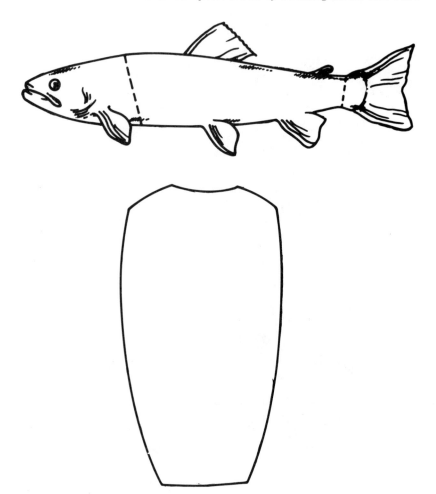

To skin a fish, make the first cut down the center back on either side of the fin. Circle the tail and just behind the head with the knife and then use your fingers or pliers to work the skin off.

To finish, immerse the skin in a solution made by combining one cup of neat's-foot oil with three cups of warm water. Put the hide to soak for about twelve hours, then remove it, drain it, wipe it dry with a cloth, and stretch it. When it is dry, remove it from the stretching board and work it over a beam until it is soft and supple. If desired, it can be pressed with a warm iron to flatten it and then sprayed with clear plastic gloss.

TANNING SNAKESKIN

Another skin that is treated like the fish skin is the snakeskin. The largest snakes make the best tanned skins, and tanned cobra skins are widely treasured and used for various articles. Rattlesnake skins are often tanned for hatbands and other decorations, and the large diamondback rattler has a particularly decorative skin.

Many people report failure when tanning snakeskins; the problem seems to be that they vary so much in thickness and quality among the species and at different seasons. Unlike mammals, snakes shed their skins every year. Since this process is ongoing, the snake's skin is terrifically thin during certain times of the year, and trying to tan it would only lead to failure.

Skinning the Snake

The first step in skinning is to cut the head off the snake and hang the body up by the tail. Using a very sharp knife, make a cut up the center of the belly from the tip of the tail to the place where the head was cut off. Using the fingers as much as possible and the knife when necessary, remove the skin from the snake's body.

Descaling and Fleshing the Skin

When the snakeskin is free of the body, wash it in clean water to remove all the loose bits of tissue, then mix up a solution made of three ounces of slaked lime in one gallon of warm water to soak it in so the scales will loosen. Be sure the lime is completely dissolved, then immerse the snakeskin in the lime water and leave it until the scales are loosened which will probably take several days.

As soon as the scales are loosened, take the hide from the lime water and use a stiff brush to brush the scales off the skin. All of the scales must be removed or the tanning solution cannot penetrate. When the scales are loosened and brushed off, be sure to flesh the skin very well, using a sharp knife carefully so you don't cut or nick the skin.

The lime must be completely removed or the tanning chemicals will be affected. This is done by soaking the skin in a neutralizing solution made by dissolving one ounce of boric acid in one gallon of warm water. Immerse the skin in this solution for about twelve hours, and then remove and rinse it in clear water.

Tanning the Skin

Now the actual tanning can start. Begin making the chrome alum mixture by mixing three ounces of salt to one gallon of water. Stir it until the salt is dissolved, and then slowly add ½ ounce of chrome alum. Continue to stir this until it is well dissolved.

Completely immerse the skin and allow it to soak for four days, moving it around two or three times a day. At the end of this time, dissolve five grams of sodium carbonate in ½ pint of warm water and add it to the tanning solution drop by drop. After the sodium has been added, soak the skin for an additional week, moving it every day.

Finally remove the skin, drain it, and soak it overnight in a solution consisting of one part sulfonated neat's-foot oil to three parts water. Remove it the next day, drain the skin, and tack it up to dry. When thoroughly dry, remove it from the board and work it over a fleshing beam until it is soft and pliable. Be careful when staking a snakeskin as it can be torn by too much pressure. If it doesn't lie flat, the skin can be ironed with an electric iron set at low heat, sprayed with clear plastic, and sewn on colored felt with pinked edges.

TANNING FROG AND LIZARD SKINS

Frog and lizard skins are also tanned, and they can be tanned with the chrome alum solution or sulfuric acid. Skins that will not be used or moved very much can be tanned with formaldehyde. Relax and flesh the skin very well, then mix four ounces of powdered borax and twenty-five drops of forty percent formaldehyde with one gallon of water. First bring the water to a boil, then take it off the heat, and while it is cooling add the borax and formaldehyde. It might require considerable stirring to dissolve the borax. Immerse the skin or skins and let them soak for about four days, moving them occasionally to make sure the solution penetrates all parts of the skin.

TANNING BIRD SKINS

One of the most gratifying projects the home tanner can embark upon is the tanning of bird skins. They can be used for wall trophies, preserved so the feathers can be used later for fly tying or feather pictures, or used for decorations on clothing and hats. To my way of thinking, the tanned and mounted skin of a game bird in full plumage is a fine trophy.

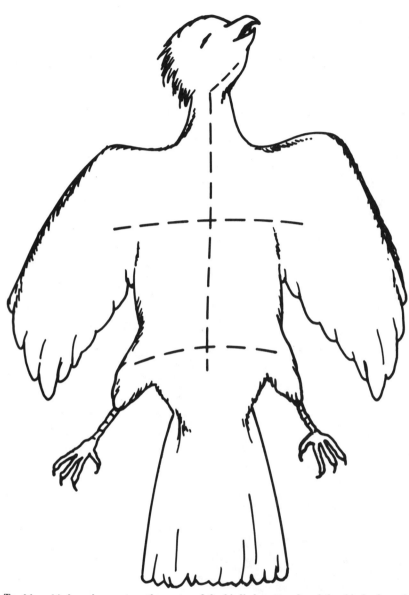

To skin a bird, make a cut up the center of the bird's breast and peel the skin back, and then cut across the wings and skin them out. Make a third cut across the legs to skin them out if this is necessary.

Skinning the Bird

Some of the bird skins that can be tanned are those of pheasants, ruffed grouse, wood ducks, and mallard drakes. Birds, like animals, skin most easily before the body heat has left them. Before you start skinning, plug up the mouth, nostrils, and vent with tufts of cotton to keep body fluids from staining the feathers during the skinning process. Then select a sharp knife with a point and make a slit from bottom beak to the vent, using your fingers to spread the feathers ahead of the knife. Many birds have a part between the feathers at this location and if you follow this line you will be cutting it in the center. Don't cut into the meat of the breast, but cut just through the skin by pushing the knife point ahead of the cut.

Ruffed grouse skins can be tanned for an eye-catching wall trophy.

Once this first slit is made you can start working the skin off away from the cut on each side. Do this with your fingers by grasping the skin in one hand and pushing on the meat with the other. Continue separating the skin from the meat, working as far as possible down the sides of the breast and toward the tail. Work the skin off around the legs and down toward the back, always pushing the meat away from the skin rather than pulling on the skin.

Once you get to the leg joints, cut them off at the knees and continue to push the tips of the fingers around the leg skin until the legs are free. There is very little fat between the skin on the bird's back and the bone, and so it is the hardest to remove. In some cases it might be necessary to push the knife point between the skin and the bone to free the skin, but care must be exercised. If a cut is made it can be sewed up to keep the feathers from protruding inside. When you get to the tailbone just cut it off and leave it on the skin. You also have to cut the gut off at this point. Use your fingers to push the meat away from the neck bones until your fingers can get all the way around it. When you reach the head, cut the neck and invert it, and then you can use the tip of the knife to cut the skin loose, using great care around the ears and eyes. Sever the beak mandibles at the head and leave the beak on the skin.

The wings are extremely hard to skin out in some birds, but they are also the most attractive part; therefore, whatever care is taken in removing the wing skin will be rewarded. I have had good luck by pushing the skin outward from the wing muscles until the wing joint is reached and severing the wing joint at this point. Usually the meat of the last joint will dry without putrifying and loosening the feathers. If you don't care to take a chance on this, inject formaldehyde with a hypodermic needle into the meat of the wing. On extra large birds, make slits under the wings and scrape away as much flesh as possible.

Tanning the Skin

It is not advisable to immerse a bird skin since the tanning fluids will mat and dull the feathers in most cases. It is better to scrape away the flesh from the skin as much as possible, and then tan it with a paste. Borax alone will keep the bird skins from rotting if they are kept in a dry place, but an alum tawing mixture will tan it very well.

Make an alum mixture by combining ½ pound of aluminum sulfate and ½ pound of salt. Add enough water to make a paste, stir it very well, let it set for one hour, and then thickly coat the flesh side of the bird skin. Cover it with a plastic sheet and let it set for two days. This will probably tan the skin, but to be on the safe side scrape off the first coat and apply a second coat. Let this stand covered for two more days, then remove the covering and let the paste dry on the skin. Scrape it off to finish the tan.

Sometimes it is desirable to tan only the breast of the bird for a wall trophy, especially when the feathers will be used for fly tying or millinery. Skin out the bird's breast by running the knife across the point of the breast and forward under the bird's wings to the neck. This will cut out a section which will include nearly all of the breast feathers. Tan the breast by stretching the feather side down on a board; then coat the flesh side with the alum paste.

If you don't intend to keep the skin more than a few weeks it only has to be dried to keep very well.

11

Making Your Tanning Tools

SKINNING AND FLESHING KNIVES

Probably the most important item for the home tanner to have is a selection of good, sharp skinning knives and an assortment of fleshing knives. Good quality skinning knives can be purchased for about twenty dollars or less, but for tanners who would like to make their own, I am describing the procedures that I use to make my knives. First go to a machine shop or factory where they use heavy-duty mechanized hacksaws and ask for any used blades that they might have on hand. These hacksaw blades wear out and have to be replaced. Made of good, high-carbon steel, they make fine knife blades or blades for fleshing knives when they are shaped.

Take the blades home and decide which one you want to use for a skinning knife. Actually, a twelve-inch blade will make two knives. Mark the blade in the center and use a carbide hacksaw blade to cut it. If you can't cut the blade, clamp it in a vise right at the cutoff mark, wrap the upper section in a rag, put a pair of safety glasses on, and strike the blade right at the vise with a hammer. This will cause it to

An industrial-type hacksaw blade that has been marked for breaking to shorten it for a knife blade.

break cleanly. The section below the vise will not be harmed, but the upper section may splinter and may have to be thrown away.

Now take the section that you want to make a knife from and lay it on the bench; then decide what shape blade you want from the illustrations shown, or use another knife that you like, and make a paper pattern of the blade and tang. Notice that the hole in the end of the blade must be centered in the tang since this is the means for attaching the handle to the blade. The back of the knife will face the teeth on the blade. Now glue the paper to the knife blade blank with a good quality glue. After the glue dries, take the blade to an electric grinder and slowly and carefully grind away all of the material in the blank that is not covered with paper. Don't let the blade get hot: if it even starts to warm up, cool it in a container of water large enough to accommodate the entire blade.

Once the blade and tang are shaped, it is time to make a handle. Although I make my handles from soft aluminum, probably the easiest way to make a handle is to saw it out of a 2 × 4 section of well-seasoned hardwood. Saw it down the center, lay the tang on each side, mark the outline of the tang on the handle, and use a wood chisel to cave out a good seat for the tang. Mark and drill a hole through the handle for fastening the tang. Finally, coat the inside of the halves of

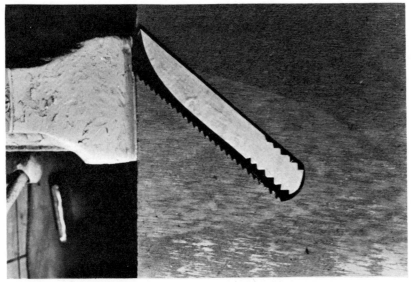

The hacksaw blade has been broken to length, and a paper cutout of the knife blade has been pasted to it for a pattern for grinding to form the knife blade and tang.

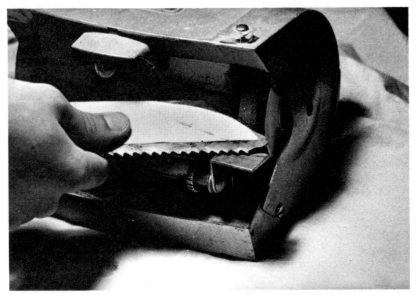

Grinding away the unneeded material in the hacksaw blade.

SKINNING KNIFE AND HANDLE

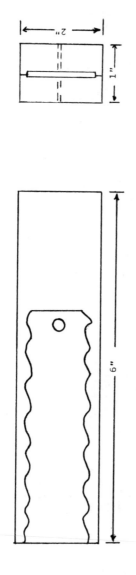

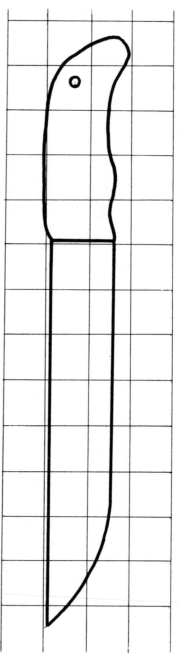

1" SQUARES

the handle with epoxy glue, put a brass bolt and nut through the hole, and draw it tight.

The wooden handle can be shaped with a wood rasp and finished with sandpaper. This is a chance to custom make a handle so it fits your hand. One way to find out what style handle fits your hand the best is to pick up other knives and try them until you find one that fits you. The handle shown in the diagram is a copy of a very popular model and will probably be satisfactory for most people.

Grinding the blade to a knife-edge and then sharpening it is a slow careful process, taking approximately two hours of time. Knife blades are ground at a 15- to 20-degree angle and they have to be sharpened slowly so the blade doesn't become overheated. However, it certainly can be done by the home do-it-yourselfer. Be sure to grind each side evenly and when it is shaped, finish sharpening it on a stone. A hacksaw knife will take a whisker-shaving edge and hold it fairly well. I use a Washita or Arkansas stone for sharpening my skinning knives.

The same type of hacksaw blades that are used to make skinning knives can be used to make fleshing knives, and fleshing blades are much easier to make. The first step is to grind the back side of the blade to a wood chisel–shaped edge of about forty-five degrees, ground from one side only. The teeth can be ground off so the back of the

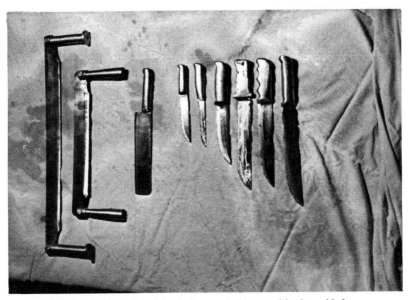

Skinning knives and fleshing knives made from used hacksaw blades.

blade is straight, or it can be left with the teeth on it for loosening flesh and fat.

The holes at the ends of the blades are used to fasten the handles on. Fine serviceable handles can be made by finding a piece of hardwood doweling, sawing off two eight-inch pieces, slotting the ends, and attaching it to the blade with stove bolts. Well-seasoned sections of oak or maple branches will work as well if commercial doweling isn't available. This completes making the skinning knife and fleshing knife, and they can be set aside while the bench, fleshing beam, slicker, and other tools are made.

TANNING BENCH

The bench is the very heart of the tanning room, and without a bench the work will be much harder. Although there are no hard and fast rules for making the bench, the one I made and use has proved satisfactory. The material list is as follows:

Material List for Tanning Bench

Four 60″ 2 × 8s for bench top.
Four 33″ 2 ×8s for bench legs.
Three 30″ 2 × 4s for cleats.
Four 27″ 2 × 4s for leg braces.*
Two 30″ 1 × 6s for cross braces on legs.

Ask the lumberyard for the following uncut lumber:
Two 10′ 2 × 8s.
One 12′ 2 × 8.
One 10′ 2 × 4, substitute two 8′ 2 × 4s for economy.
One 8′ 2 × 4.
One 8′ 1 × 6.

Additional Materials:
1 pound of 6d nails.
1 pound of 8d nails.
1 pound of 10d nails.
2 pounds of 16d nails.
1 quart of exterior paint.
*Be sure to measure the distance before cutting these.

First saw the 10-foot 2 × 8s in half to produce four 5-foot lengths. (A) (See Tanning Bench illustration.) Next saw two of the 8-foot 2 ×

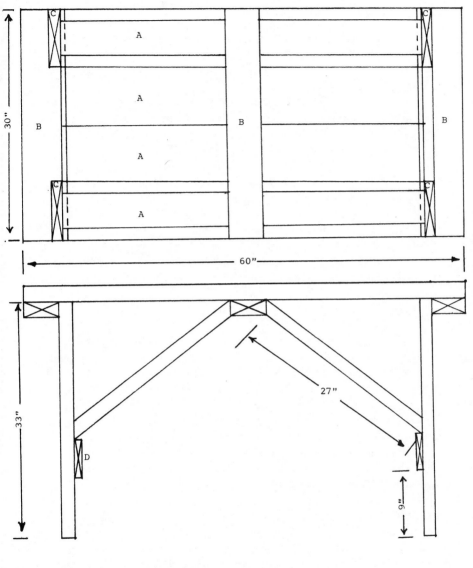

TANNING BENCH

4s in half to produce three sections of 2 × 4 for braces. (B) Find a hammer and a handful of 8d nails and lay out the 2 × 8s on a level surface so the ends are even. Lay the 2 × 4 braces across the 2 × 8s in the proper position and nail through the 2 × 4 to fasten the 2 × 8s together to form the table top which measures about 60 inches by 30 inches.

Now saw four 33-inch sections from the 2 × 8 stock for legs. (C) Position them correctly as shown and nail through the legs into the 2 × 4 leg braces using 8d nails. Next, saw out two sections of 1 × 6 which measure about 2 feet long. (D) Use 6d nails to nail the 1 × 10s to the legs using five nails to each board positioned in a box pattern for maximum strength. The final step is to saw out the braces which extend from the legs to the center, cutting them on a 45-degree angle. Fasten the braces to the legs and top using 10d nails. To finish the bench, set it up on its legs and nail down through the top into the end grain of each leg with two 16d nails. Paint the bench with at least two coats of good wood paint to resist decay and prevent contamination from the animal matter that it will be in contact with.

FLESHING BEAMS

With the bench completed, the smaller equipment that will be used with the bench can be constructed. At least three sizes of fleshing beams will be convenient, the smallest being useful for fleshing small animals about the size of a squirrel or weasel to a large mink. Make this beam from a piece of 4-inch diameter hardwood stock about 6 feet long. Study the diagram for the proper shape. To use the fleshing beam, nail a U-shaped bracket to the side of the bench and place the fleshing beam in the bracket so one end is on the floor.

The second beam is the one that can be used for everything from a skunk to a coyote, and it is also used in conjunction with the bench. Although most fleshing beams are shown as being placed in an inclined position so the operator bends over and pushes his fleshing knife forward, some tanners think the level beam is the most comfortable to work with, especially when long hours must be spent fleshing hides. Because the bench has a tendency to slide across the floor during fleshing, push the bench against a wall before you start. If you don't care to bolt the beam to the bench, it can be used by placing it over a sawhorse with one end against the wall. By fastening a larger bracket to the side of the bench, the fleshing beam can also be used in a vertical position. The demountable stand shown in the drawing is adjustable

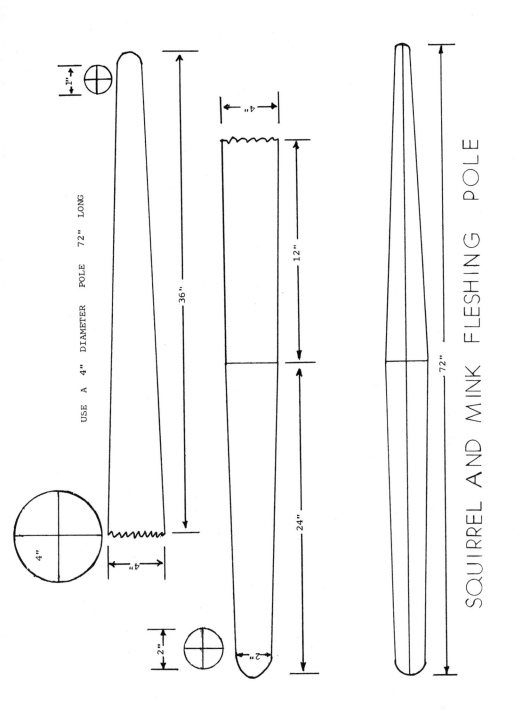

USE A 4" DIAMETER POLE 72" LONG

36"

4"

4"

2"

4"

12"

24"

2"

72"

SQUIRREL AND MINK FLESHING POLE

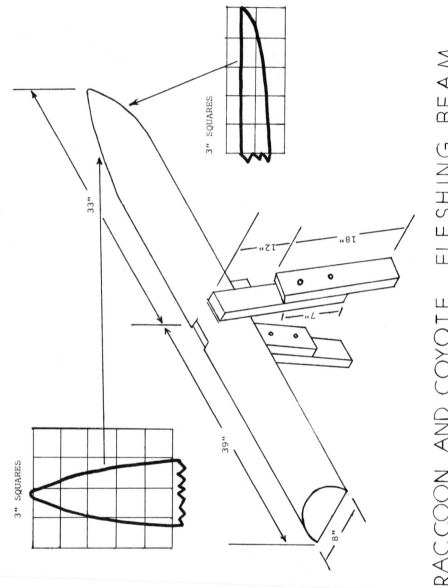

3" SQUARES

3" SQUARES

33"

39"

12"

18"

7"

8"

RACCOON AND COYOTE FLESHING BEAM

for different heights. The fleshing beam can be removed from the stand so it can be stored against the wall out of the way when it isn't in use.

One of the most economical ways to make this fleshing beam is to obtain an 8-inch diameter or larger hardwood log. Cut it to 6 feet in length, and then split or saw it in half with a chain saw. Set one half aside to be used for the deerskin fleshing beam. Now take the other half and lay it at a comfortable height on a bench and mark out the proper tapered shape for the beam as shown on the drawing. Saw out this shape, turn the log over and layout the lines to thin the ends of the log, and saw these out also. A chain saw or coarse-toothed handsaw can be used for these cuts. When the rough shape is sawed out, use a draw knife or large butcher knife to shave the tapered end of the beam to the proper shape. Finally, sand it very smooth since any nicks could cause the hide to be damaged under the fleshing knife. The demountable stand is made from 2 × 4 stock or small poles.

The deerskin tanning beam can be made from the other half of the log. All that is necessary is to shave the knots from half the beam and sand it smooth. Saw a notch in the beam where it fits against the bench and place the butt end against a wall so it doesn't slip.

Nearly the same procedure is used to make a beam from a 6-foot section of 2 × 8 milled lumber except the edges of the board must be shaved or sanded to a rounded shape that will fit a curved fleshing knife. Even if a straight-blade fleshing knife is used, the rounded corners prevent the hide from being cut on the edge of the boards.

Hides are pulled over the beam with fur side in and fleshed downward, from head to tail. For tanning, all flesh and fat should be completely removed and a well-made beam will make this process easier and more effective.

For cattle or horse hides, a large diameter fleshing beam is a great convenience. Although they can be scraped or fleshed on a flat surface, the work is nearly twice as hard as when they are fleshed on a rounded beam. A wooden barrel laid on its side on wooden blocks to raise it up to a convenient height can also be used for fleshing large hides. Just be sure no sharp edges are extending up from the metal barrel hoops, and have the bottom of the barrel pushed against the wall or other immovable object.

However, to equip our tanning room for extensive work on large hides, it is expedient to make up a professional tanner's beam. It can be made by the home workman without any special tools. First, go to a salvage lumber outlet and get ten 6-foot sections of 1 × 4 tongue and groove hardwood flooring and an 8-foot 2 × 6. When you get home, cut the 2 × 6 into pieces as shown on the drawing and nail each two

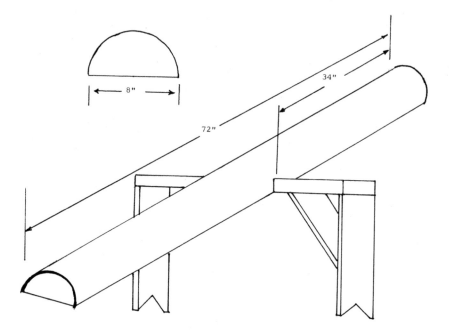

DEER SKIN FLESHING BEAM

Material List For Large Skins Fleshing Beam:
Ten 8' tongue and groove 1 × 4s.*
Two 48" 2 × 6s for the legs.
Two 24" 2 × 6s for each cross section. Six required.
Two 24" 2 × 4s. Six required.
*A section of ¼-inch, exterior grade, finished-on-one-side plywood can be used as an alternative.

sections of the 2 × 6s together to form two 11 × 24 sections. Lay out the radius as shown on the drawing and saw out two half moon–shaped forming frames. When these are done, nail the tongue and groove lumber to the frames to form the half round tanner's beam.

Start nailing at the radius of the 2 × 8 frames, and continue nailing alternately on each side of the starter board. Use 8d nails driven at an angle to push the tongue and groove joints together as well as possible. Some spreading of the joints will occur but they will not deter from the efficient use of the tanner's beam. When it is finished it should be sanded to remove all splinters, and all nail heads should be countersunk. No paint is necessary.

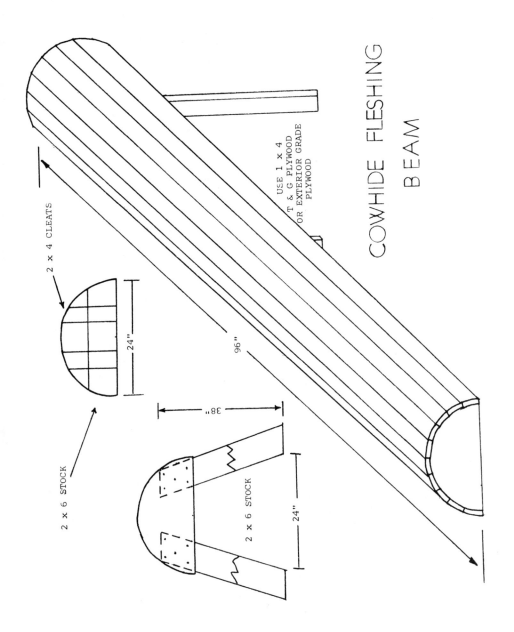

COWHIDE FLESHING

BEAM

2 x 4 CLEATS

USE 1 x 4
T & G PLYWOOD
OR EXTERIOR GRADE
PLYWOOD

2 x 6 STOCK

24"

38"

2 x 6 STOCK

24"

96"

One end can be raised to a convenient height for working by setting it on a sawhorse. If it is to be left in one place most of the time, the legs can be made from 2 × 6s. The beam should be about thirty-three inches high at the raised end.

WOODEN AND METAL EDGE SLICKERS

The slicker, an important piece of tanning equipment, is used for pushing the water and grease out of the skin and softening it. It is made from a piece of 2 × 6 hardwood lumber measuring about 6 inches. If a table saw is available, saw a section of the board measuring 6 inches, then cut it into a wedge shape with the apex ⅜ inch thick. Use a plane to shape the thicker edge to a rounded shape and finish by sanding it. The working edge should be about ¼ inch thick when it is finished and smoothed; the part that is kept in your hands can be maintained about 1½ inches thick.

Another way to make a slicker is to set a 6-inch section of ¼- × - 2-inch thick strap iron in a wooden handle so the working edge protrudes about one inch. This can be done by sawing an inch deep slot in the edge of a 6-inch board, sliding the strap iron into the slot, and bolting it in. Drill ¼-inch holes through the boards and strap iron in place. File the working edge of the strap iron so it is rounded and smooth, being careful to round off the corners.

STAKE

Another piece of equipment that can be easily made at home is the stake for softening the leather. It is made from an 8-inch board about 3 feet long if it is going to be used standing up. The top end should be tapered to a fairly sharp edge, about ¼ inch thick, and it should be sanded smooth, with the corners rounded. It will be held in an upright position by brackets bolted to the side of the bench, or it can be clamped in a vise. It can be placed in the bracket that is used for the medium-sized fleshing beam.

If you don't have a bench to work with, make up a board 4 feet long and taper the ends as described. Nail it to a base and brace it well so it will withstand the forces that the softening process involves. A tanner that will only be tanning one skin could sink a pole in the ground in the same way as a fence post is set, and then the top could be shaped with a chain or handsaw and sanded smooth. As an alternative, a board that was sawed and sanded to a tapered edge could be bolted to the side of the tanning bench and used for a stake.

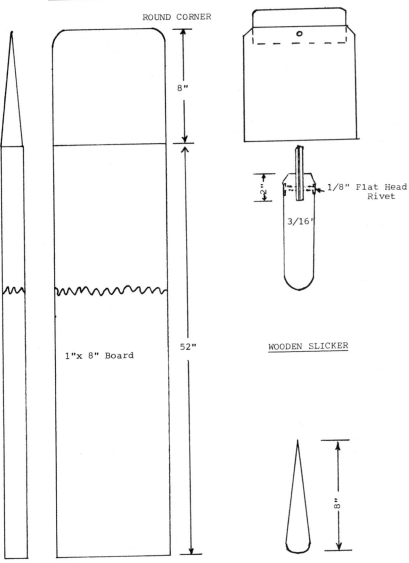

SKIN STAKE

METAL EDGE SLICKER

ROUND CORNER

8"

1"x 8" Board

52"

1/8" Flat Head
Rivet

3/16"

WOODEN SLICKER

8"

Material List:
One 15′ 1 × 8 board for skin stake.
One 8′ 1 × 8 board for wooden slicker.
One 8″ 1 × 8 board, 6″ ⅛ × 4 metal stock, and 1⅛ × 1 flathead rivet for metal edge slicker.

BREAKING BENCH

A device that serious home tanners will find useful is the breaking or pulling bench. This bench is used to soften and break down the skin fibers so the skin will soak up oil and become soft and supple. It consists of a bench for the operator to sit on and a blade fastened in a vertical position placed in front of the operator. It is used by pulling the skin across the sharpened edge of the blade. The edge of the blade is kept fairly sharp because it takes a thin edge to create the sharp pressure necessary to soften the skin. Because skins can be damaged if they are pulled too hard against the blade or if it slides vertically during the pulling operation, a piece of low value skin should be used for practice before expensive skins are "broken."

Start making the bench by cutting a 42-inch section of 2 × 12. Saw a slot in one end about 3/16 inch wide or as wide as two saw blade cuts and extend ten to twelve inches into the board. The breaking blade will rest in this slot and the slot has to be long enough to allow the blade to pivot when it is adjusted. As shown on the drawing, drill a

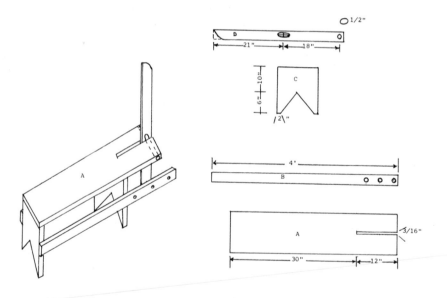

BREAKING BENCH

Material List for Breaking Bench:
A. 2″ × 10″ × 42″
B. Two 2 × 4 × 48s
C. Two 2 × 10 × 16s
D. One 3″ × 42″ flat stock

⅜-inch hole one inch from the slotted end to retain the pivot bolt for the blade.

Next saw out the bench legs as shown on the drawing and then obtain and cut the 2 × 4 side braces. They are cut to 48-inch lengths and ½-inch holes are drilled through the 2 × 4s as shown to receive a 14-inch section of ⅜-inch ready bolt, which is used to adjust the angle of the breaking blade. The exact position of the ½-inch holes can best be found after the bench is set up since it will vary according to the size of the operator. However, if the holes are drilled at two-inch intervals starting two inches from the end of the 2 × 4s, proper adjustment for almost any operator can be realized. The most expedient way to drill the holes is to clamp the 2 × 4s together before they are nailed to the bench and then to drill through both boards at the same time.

The breaking blade can be made from ¼- × -3-inch or wider steel flat stock. If a used, cross-cut saw blade is available it can be shaped into a fine breaking blade by cutting off the teeth and sharpening one edge to a knife-edge. The blade is mounted on the bench so the sharp edge faces away from the operator, and the blade is drilled one inch from the lower end for the bottom bolt. A slot approximately ½ inch wide and 2 inches long is cut into the blade approximately eighteen inches above the bottom bolt hole which allows the blade to be adjusted on the bench. After the blade is nailed on the bench and adjusted properly, it can be sharpened with a file to about the sharpness of a fleshing knife. As the operator gains experience he may be able to sharpen it still further which will speed up the work somewhat.

Where it is not expedient to build a pulling bench, the blade can be fastened to a work bench at a height that is favorable to either standing or sitting in a chair while doing the pulling. With the work bench we built in this chapter, the blade can be fastened to a 2 × 4 bolted horizontally across the legs. In this case two ½-inch holes are drilled through the blade and matching holes are drilled through the 2 × 4 so the blade can be placed on whatever slant is desired for work.

12

Primitive Tanning Methods

TANNING HISTORY

People have been tanning hides since long before recorded history. Probably the cave dwellers quickly learned that the skins they wore could be smoked or treated with various natural substances to preserve them and keep them soft and flexible. The Egyptians made leather that was so well preserved some specimens over 3,000 years old are still in almost perfect condition. The Egyptians and Hebrews recorded many of the tanning methods of the ancients dating back 5,000 years. The early Greeks and Romans contributed much to the science of tanning and some of their methods are still used. The word "tan" was coined by the Romans who used leather as a basis for money.

Drawings in a cave near Teruel, Spain show women dressed in fur coats and skirts, and other drawings in caves in the Spanish Pyrenees show men wearing fur boots and trousers. These drawings are thought to be over 20,000 years old.

Tanning was a highly regarded enterprise in the old world, and methods for producing good leather were closely guarded and passed on from generation to generation. Until the middle of the nineteenth century almost all leather was tanned with vegetable tannins. The heavy leather was spread out in pits, and layers of bark, leaves, and fruits of various plants were spread over the leather. Water was gradually added as the pit filled. The water leached the tannin from the vegetation and then it combined with the hide to tan it. This process took months or even years to complete if the leather was a heavy cowhide or horsehide.

Potash-alum appears to be the next tanning agent that the ancients discovered, particularly the people of the Middle East. The Greeks were using this method by 450 A.D. and the Assyrians, Babylonians, and Sumerians were known to be skilled in its use. In one method the leather was also pasted with ground gall nuts and concentrated grape juice which is a combination of vegetable and mineral tanning—a method widely practiced today.

Alum-tanned leather is white and takes dye well; the Egyptians dyed their leather beautiful shades of red, yellow, blue, and black with plant dye. In the eighteenth century Spanish or cordovan leather was developed in Spain, and it was either pure white or red and was world famous. But, it wasn't until the nineteenth century that it was introduced into Britain where alum-tanned leather was hailed as a major innovation. The chief negative quality of alum-tanned leather is that the alum is soluble in water and if the leather is soaked in water long enough or repeatedly the alum will be gone and the leather will get stiff and start to decay.

No more major innovations were recorded in the leather-making process until about 1880 when a corset manufacturer in the United States complained to his leather supplier, August Schultz, that the alum-tanned leather was causing the metal stays in women's corsets to corrode. He complained to the right man because Schultz was an experienced textile dyer and was familiar with bi-chromate mordants which were used to fix dye in clothing. Schultz and his friends started experimenting with a tanning process that was similar to alum tanning but which used the substance chrome-alum instead of potash-alum as a tanning agent. They finally discovered that the chrome solution could be fixed with soda ash and salt into an agent that would tan as well as potash-alum and had the advantage of not leaching out in water or perspiration. This extremely good tanning method is used for most leather today.

In 1945 it was discovered that acetone could be substituted for water and some tanning processes could be done in minutes instead of hours. This is used in commercial tanning operations, though it is probably not adaptable or necessary for the home tanner.

Modern day tanneries are marvels of efficiency, and although they have to go through the same steps as the home tanner, the fleshing, beaming, and tumbling are done by machine. A skilled chemist is at hand to keep the different substances in the right proportions.

INDIAN TANNING METHODS

It is interesting to note that most of the methods used in the leather industry are simply mechanical adaptations of the American Indian methods of producing leather from deer, buffalo, and elk hides. The American Indians tanned all hides in about the same way. Some were so skillful that they could turn a deerskin into a suit of clothes within forty-eight hours of the time the deer was killed.

The Indians removed the hair from the skins by immersing them in a log container filled with water and wood ashes. If a hollow log wasn't available, they dug a hole in the ground, placed the skin to be dehaired flesh side down in the hole so the skin would be a waterproof bag. Any holes in the skin were sewn up so the hide wouldn't leak water, and then wood ashes and water were placed in the skin bag. The lye produced by the ashes and water would hasten the decomposition of the epidermis layer of skin and loosen the hair. Usually the skin could be dehaired in three to four days. Sometimes a paste of wood ashes and water was rubbed repeatedly into the hair side of the skin to loosen the hair. However, about the simplest way was to immerse the skin in a brook or pond and leave it until the hair loosened.

Once the hair was very loose, the Indians would scrape it off using the inner front leg bone of the deer as a scraper. This bone was also used as a fleshing tool, and that was the next step after the hair was removed. They spent considerable amount of time removing every bit of flesh and membrane from the hide. Extra tough material had to be removed with a clam shell or a sharp stone. A smooth, peeled log was used for a fleshing beam, and for staking the hide some Indians used a sapling that was formed into a sharp edge so the hide could be sawed back and forth over it. Usually the hide was staked several times during the tanning process to soften it.

As soon as the deer was butchered, the brains and liver were slowly cooked together to make the tanning substance. When the skin was properly dehaired and fleshed, it was stretched on a pole frame and the brains and liver were rubbed into it. This operation was repeated three or four times to make sure the hide was well lubricated with tannin. Each time it was taken down from the frame it was either staked with a sharpened stump and rubbed with clam shells or stones until it was soft and supple. This took at least three treatments to make a nice, soft skin.

When the skin was just right, a process that the Indians took great pride in, it was smoked over a slow fire of punky or green wood for three or four days until the smoke completely penetrated the hide and turned it a tan or brown color.

Traditionally Tanning Buckskin

We can make buckskin today very quickly and easily by adapting the Indian's methods to what we have available now. Buckskin tanned this way won't be the equal of chrome- or vegetable-tanned leather, but it will be soft, beautiful, and useful if made right. It also can be made quickly and easily. This method will also tan calf, coyote, sheep, or goat skins as well as deer, antelope, or elk skin.

First skin the animal and let the hide cool. If you obtain a skin from a hunter or dealer the hide has probably been salted and rolled up. If the hide is salted or stiff, soak it overnight to wash out the salt or relax it. Then mix up a dehairing solution made by dissolving ¼ cup of lye in ten gallons of water and continue to soak the skin in this solution until the hair loosens. This probably won't take more than twelve hours in warm weather, but leave it long enough so the hide can be easily scraped very clean.

Use an inclined log or board for a fleshing beam and scrape the hide free of all hair and dirt. Rinse the skin in clear water and flesh it very well, removing every bit of flesh and fat. In Indian tanning, this is about the most important part of the tanning procedure.

When it is well fleshed, soak it in clear water, stirring and kneading it well before letting it soak overnight. The next morning, remove the skin from the water and wring the water out by twisting it. One way to do this is to throw the skin over a tree limb so both sides dangle about evenly. Tie the dangling ends together with stout rope or rawhide, put a broomstick or similar handle through the loop of skin, and twist it to tighten the skin into a rope shape. Maintain the tension on the skin by wedging the broomstick against the tree trunk; leave the skin in this position until it stops dripping water. This will probably take eight hours or more.

Then untwist the skin, and either pull it out or tack it tightly on a stretching frame so it regains its original shape.

Commercial tanning oil, lard, or neat's-foot oil can be used as a tanning liquid. A common and economical product that will produce a good tan is Fel-Naptha soap. To prepare the soap, shave two bars into a pint jar, fill the jar with hot water, and stir it until the soap is dissolved. Set aside to let it cool. The find a five-gallon plastic or wooden container and pour enough warm (130° F.) water in it to cover the skin. Stir the soap into the mixture, place the skin in the solution, make sure it is completely submerged, and let it soak for four to five days. It should be stirred four times a day if possible.

In five days take the skin out of the soap solution, discard the soap, and twist the skin over the limb again to wring it out. When it quits dripping, remove it from the limb, and either stretch it on a frame or by hand as it dries so it doesn't shrink too much. When it has dried to the damp stage, smear it with a thick coating of lard, bacon grease, butter, or melted tallow.

Next, make up a new batch of soap suds and immerse the skin again. Let it soak three more days, stirring it often. Finally, take it out of the soap suds, rinse it well, twist it to drain, and then work it over a stake or stretch it as it dries. When it is at the damp stage, tack it to a stretching frame and let it dry. It also should be protected from freezing cold weather, sun, and high artificial temperatures.

Now the skin can be staked until it is soft and supple. If it has dried stiff, it will probably have to be dampened by rolling it up in a damp cloth before it can be worked over the stake. If needed, a light coating of neat's-foot oil can be applied during the staking procedure.

When this is done to your satisfaction, the hide should be smoked. Use a very small, smoky fire of punky wood. Make up a small tepee frame that the hide will cover. The hide also can be hung in a smokehouse or it can be dangled in an inverted barrel. Dig a trench from the barrel to a fire pit a few feet away. This will insure that the heat from the fire doesn't contact the skin since heat will ruin it. Smoking will make the hide partially waterproof and color it. If the buckskin dries out somewhat stiff after it has been wet, just rub it with your hands until it is soft and dry.

Traditionally Tanning Rawhide

Second to tanned deerskin, rawhide was probably the most useful item that the Indians and early settlers could make. The uses are nearly endless: Rawhide makes fine buckets, boxes, gun cases, knife sheaths, bags, buttons, leggings, chaps, and it can be used to mend broken gun stocks and knife handles. It was utilized for door hinges, windows, laces, bindings, snowshoes, and nearly everything else that nails, wire, and string are used for today. One of the greatest assets of rawhide is the way it shrinks after it is wetted. This quality was utilized for bonding handles, forming tight chair seat fits, making clothing with water resistant seams, and hundreds of other uses.

Rawhide can be formed from most any skin, depending upon its anticipated use. If it will be used mostly for containers, the heavy hides can be used. For general purposes, any animal hide, or a hide that is rubbed or otherwise unsuitable for tanning, can be used.

A skin that will be made into rawhide should not be salted; instead, soften it with water and immerse it in a dehairing solution made by combining 2½ pounds of slaked caustic lime with ten gallons of water. Leave it in the solution until the hair slips very easily, and then remove it and rinse it in clean water. After letting it drain, put it on the fleshing beam and scrape off the hair and the epidermis layer of skin under the hair. When the hair is gone, turn the hide over and flesh it very well, removing every bit of flesh and fat. Then soak it for awhile in clean water to wash away all dirt and bits of material removed by the fleshing and dehairing operations.

Next, stretch the hide as tightly as you can by hand and either tack it down to a flat surface or punch holes around the perimeter and lace it inside a frame. The rawhide is left on the frame until it dries, then it is rolled up and stored in a cool, dry place. Before it is used, it has to be softened in water.

If the rawhide is cut into strips for laces or other uses, this can be done in several ways, but the pioneer method was to drive a nail in a piece of board and then drive a sharp knife beside it the width of the thong to be made. Take the piece of rawhide and make an inch long cut in the edge of the rawhide the width of the lace to be made. Feed the two ends between the nail and knife blade, grasping the ends and pulling them through. This will continue cutting the same width lace. Any length lace can be made this way by working with a circular piece. Just keep turning the piece and shaving a lace from the perimeter until the entire circle is used up. A 4½-inch diameter piece can yield two boot laces if cut this way.

Some people can do a very good job of cutting laces with a pair of scissors, but remember that the lace is only as strong as its weakest part. If you cut one section narrower than the other, it should be cut at the point. Then either start over with a new lace, knot it at that point, or use glue to hold it together. Woodchuck, summer raccoon, and eel skins were widely used for boot laces. Before using the boot laces, heat some neat's-foot oil until it is warm to the touch, and immerse the laces in it overnight.

Primitive Tanning Projects

Rawhide boxes, lens covers, buckets, baskets, and many other items can be made by stretching a soaked hide over a wooden frame and letting it dry. After thick rawhide dries, it is nearly as hard as iron and almost as indestructible.

Rawhide was often made into hats by primitive people. First a section of thick rawhide was soaked in water until it was soft. While it was soaking, a hat mold was made by digging a hole in the ground of the right size, using an old hat for a pattern. The hole was flattened around the edges for the brim, and the wet rawhide was fitted into the hole. The inside of the hat was filled with sand, and the rawhide was weighted to the flattened area by covering it with sand also.

After the hat was well dried, it was removed from the mold and trimmed. If it didn't fit the wearer's head comfortably it was dampened and reshaped slightly. When it was perfectly shaped, it was smoked until it was waterproof.

Rawhide and objects made from rawhide will be eaten by dogs and other animals unless they are treated with mineral oil or another preservative. They also can be rubbed with taxidermist's paste to make them unpalatable to all predators.

Primitive people also made extensive use of buffalo or elk robes tanned with the hair on. To make a robe by the Indian method, flesh the raw skin very well, and stretch it on a 4 × 8 section of ½-inch plywood. Use 8d nails to take the skin down with, placing them about an inch apart all around the skin. Move the skin to the top of the nails so air can circulate between the hair and the plywood.

Let the hide stay on the frame until it dries hard. Then use an electric sander, hand sander, or rasp to thin the hide to ⅛ inch (eight ounces) or less in thickness, if necessary. Blow or brush off all debris and then coat the skin with a soap solution made by dissolving two bars of Fel-Naptha soap in two cups of hot water. Brush this on the skin, rub it in well, and let it sit until it soaks in. If the skin is too dry to absorb the solution, sprinkle it with warm water, cover the flesh side, and let it set overnight. The next morning it should be damp and ready to absorb the soap.

Apply three successive coats of soap, applying the next one as soon as the last has soaked in, and then take the skin off the frame and smoke it. If it is too stiff to handle well, damped it and work it over a breaking knife or tumble it in a clothes dryer until it is flexible. Smoke the robe over a small punky fire in the same way that the deerskin was smoked. When it is well smoked it can be softened to whatever degree is desired by rubbing oil into it and tumbling or working it over a breaking edge.

The Indians and pioneers used nearly every animal and bird in the forest for various purposes. Animals the size of a fox or smaller were used for bags and containers of all sorts. One important part of tanning them was the way the small animals were skinned. The entire carcass was removed by working it out through the animal's mouth, turning the animal inside out as it was skinned, and producing a skin without any holes except for the mouth and anus. It was then fleshed very well and a mixture of brains and liver were rubbed into the skin. Afterwards it was staked over a sharp stake driven in the ground or a sinew rope that was tied between two trees about five feet apart. The skin was also smoked to make it water resistant, and the mouth of the skin was fitted with laces so it could be pulled tight. This produced a very useful, long-lived, and decorative container.

Primitive living buffs can do the same thing, but it is now much easier. A muskrat is a good animal to use. First dry the hair if the animal is wet and then slit the mouth back on each side of the head. Use a sharp knife to carefully skin out the head, pulling the legs out of the skin as you move backward. Pliers and a large spoon are handy for pulling the flesh and bones forward through the head opening.

Flesh the skin when you have it all turned inside out and mix up a sulfuric acid tanning solution made by combining one pound of salt and four ounces of automotive-type battery acid with one gallon of water. Except for the mouth, sew up any openings in the skin, and fill the skin with the solution through the mouth. Hang the skin head side up and let it hang for up to five days or until it tans through to the outside. This can be ascertained by a change in skin appearance.

Then dump the tanning solution out of the skin, rinse it well, and fill it again with a solution made by dissolving one ounce of baking soda in one gallon of water to neutralize the acid. Fill the skin, let it stand for two hours, dump out this first bath, and fill it again. Let this stand for two more hours, dump it out, and then rinse the skin with clear water. After it is rinsed, turn the skin flesh side out and let it dry to the damp stage. Then fill the skin with sawdust, and tamp it down very well so it expands the skin to a bag shape. Hang it up and let it dry. Then dump out the sawdust and the skin is ready to use for a container. Cut slits in the head area for lacing a tie string so the opening can be pulled shut.

Many skins are tanned by immersing them in a wet poultice of oak leaves, oak galls, oak bark, hemlock bar, or even tea leaves. This is vegetable tan and if the process is done correctly it is a very fine tan.

First flesh the skin very well. Then for a skin the size of a squirrel skin, fill a gallon container full of alfalfa leaves, oak leaves, bark, galls, or other high tannin vegetable matter. Heat a gallon of water to the boiling point and pour it over the vegetable material. Let it steep overnight and the next morning immerse the skin in the center of the tanning container. Leave the skin in the tanning solution for at least two weeks, stirring it every day. When it is well tanned, the brown color of the tanning solution will have penetrated the thickness of the skin. Remove and dry the skin; then oil and stake as you would any other skin.

13

Using Your Leather

Many outdoorsmen derive tremendous satisfaction from hunting or trapping a wild animal, tanning its hide, and then turning the leather into a vest, pair of mittens, or other long lasting and useful item. Domestic animal skins are also interesting to work with, and a huge business in selling tanned hides to home craftsmen is enjoyed by large chains of leather outlets.

TYPES, GRADES, AND AVAILABILITY OF LEATHER

Each type of leather project has a skin that is best suited to it, but before the beginner can make a shrewd selection he must consider the basic qualities of leather. Each species of animal has a hide of different thickness which also varies during the seasons of the year. Summer skin is thicker than winter skin. However, in commercial tanneries, hides are "split" to a uniform thickness and then graded by weight per square foot.

One-ounce leather is $\frac{1}{64}$ inch thick; two to three ounce leather is $\frac{1}{32}$ inch thick; four to five ounce leather is $\frac{1}{16}$ inch thick; six to eight ounces is ³⁄₃₂ inches thick; and ³⁄₁₆ leather weighs nine to twelve ounces to the square foot. Each ¹⁄₆₄ inch thickness of leather weighs one ounce more.

The home tanner will be working with skins of natural thickness, and he can expect sheepskin and rabbit skin to be one ounce or heavier, deerskin to be two ounces or heavier, and cowhide to be up to twelve ounces. The hide from an old cow can be thicker than any other domestic hide, including horsehide. The thinnest skins are the most flexible and softest, but most any skin can be made soft and flexible by the proper tanning, shaving, and staking.

The location on the animal's body also indicates a certain quality of leather. Large hides are divided into sections called bends, shoulders, bellies, and heads. The bends which are sections of hide on either side of the backbone from the rump to the shoulders are considered to be the finest because they are even, durable, and have a smooth texture. Shoulders are second in quality. They are fine leather but they often contain wrinkles. Bellies place last because they are loose and stretchy. Heads are good quality but they are small and uneven.

The tanning method imparts various qualities to the leather as do the finishing agents. Generally leathers that are oil tanned are soft, supple, and stretchy. Chrome-tanned leathers are somewhat waterproof, and they will stretch and stay stretched. Vegetable-tanned leathers are the most versatile since they can be tooled, molded, and finished

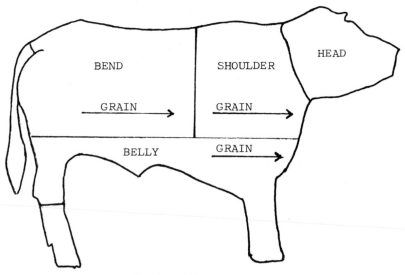

How large hides are sectioned.

to be waterproof. They also can be stretched when wet and they will not shrink again when they dry. Vegetable-tanned leathers take dye and other finishes very well.

It is useful to examine the characteristics of the hides from different animals. Cowhide is the most common leather. The skin from bulls, calves, unborn calves, and cows is called cowhide. In addition to being uniform, durable, and very workable, cowhides are also the most easily available skins since they can be obtained from farmers at butchering time or from numerous slaughterhouses.

Equine hides from horses, mules, and donkeys also make good leather or rugs and are often more durable than cowhide.

Sheepskin is thin and strong. It is widely used in wool-on and wool-off projects. Goatskin is also very adaptable, but goats are relatively rare in United States. Pigskin from domestic hogs is often used for some projects, but it is inferior to other leathers. However, wild pigskin makes very good glove and fancy leather.

Deerskin is soft and supple yet quite strong, and it can be used for most any garment. It has a less complicated cell structure than other animals and therefore is easily tanned. Elk and moose hides are usually thicker than deerskin and usually have to be split or shaved down before they can be used. Many tanners consider both hides to be inferior to deerskin.

In the commercial tanning process, almost all cowhides are split by machine into uniform thicknesses before they are used. The layers shaved off are called "splits" and they are rough on both sides. Splits are usually used for suede leather, and the top layer, called "top grain," is the most valuable. All commercial leather is dyed after being tanned, and some is plated to give it a smooth finish or embossed with different patterns.

Commercial tanners often grade their leather as A, B, C, D, X, or 1, 2, 3, 4, 5, with A or #1 leather being the most valuable. These numbers have no bearing on the wearing quality of leather, instead they refer to the number of imperfections in the leather. Although A grade leather is the most expensive, the home leather crafter can often use C or D grade leather and obtain the same results since he can cut around the imperfections in the leather far easier than commercial leather makers can stamp out the pieces for a pattern.

Home workers can usually save money by buying a side of cowhide which will run about twenty-two to twenty-six square feet. The next size is calfhide which runs about nine to fifteen square feet to the complete hide. Calfhides are also sold by the half which is called a kip. Sheep and goat hides run about five to nine square feet, deerskins about seven to nine square feet, and pigskins average ten to fourteen square feet. Moosehides are usually split into sides, and the sides are generally smaller than cowhides. Elk hides are also available which average twelve to fourteen feet to the hide. Antelope skins are often tanned, but the leather is considered inferior. Many specialty skins are available also such as alligator, snake, frog, kangaroo, and ostrich.

Cowhide can be used for everything from shoe soles to gloves; horsehide is usually only used for harnesses and similar projects; deerhide is used for garments and gloves; goat hides are often used for lacing and billfold liners; while sheepskin is used for shirts, jackets, wool on slippers and jackets, and many other projects. Snake, alligator, and frog skins are usually used for facing on leather belts, purses, wallets, and shoes.

PROJECTS IN LEATHER

Probably the most expedient method of calculating the amount of leather you will need for a certain project is to acquire or develop the pattern. Patterns are available from many leather-working shops or a cloth pattern can be used by increasing the seam width to an inch. If you already have a cloth garment that you want to duplicate in leather, just rip out the seams of the cloth garment. Iron them so they lay flat and use the pieces for the pattern. Just remember to make the seams wider (they can be trimmed) and make the sleeves, pants, and legs one inch longer since leather tends to bunch up at the knees and elbows. Carefully measure the pattern, figure the increase, add about fifteen percent for waste, and you have the correct figure for the amount of leather you need for a project.

Leather-Working Tools

Although you can make several simple leather projects with just a knife, scissors, a hammer, and a nail, it will be helpful to acquire a few specialized leather-working tools. Leather can be cut easily with a utility knife; these knives have interchangeable blades, or they can be sharpened with a few strokes on the sharpening stone. It is easier to follow a line with the utility knife than with a kitchen or hunting knife. The awl is useful for making lines or for marking for later punching of holes. Revolving punches can be used to make different sized holes in leather for sewing, placing rivets or laces, or other uses. When leather is cut with a utility knife, the cut edge is square. A tool called an edge beveler rounds the edges, making it look more polished.

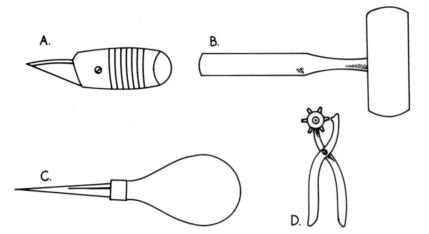

Tools for leather working: (A) utility knife (B) mallet (C) awl (D) revolving punch.

A wooden or rawhide mallet is more convenient than a metal hammer when working with leather as it won't damage the leather's surface. Needles are needed for most projects. Leather needles are available, but any two-inch needle with a large eye will do.

The leather worker also can use dyes, daubers, glue, cement, thread, and saddle soap or paste wax. Sooner or later you will also need rings, buckles, snaps, and rivets. These objects are called findings, and they are made of a variety of metals ranging from solid brass, brass plated, nickle plated, copper, pewter, or white metal. Solid metal findings are more expensive, but the finish will not wear off as it will from plated findings.

Now, with the leather, pattern, and tools assembled, the actual leather working can begin. Be sure to make a pattern for each piece of leather even if the pieces are identical because the thought that goes into making a pattern can help prevent mistakes in the cutting.

In all cases, make a fabric or heavy paper dummy of your project before you cut your valuable leather. After leather is cut it is very hard to correct errors.

When all of your pattern pieces are made, roll out the leather on a tabletop with the grain side up and inspect it. If it has deep cuts, spots, or thin places, make a mental note of them. Then turn the leather over, flesh side up, and lay the pattern pieces on the leather. To make maximum use of your leather, work inward from one edge with the pattern pieces laying edge to edge so little or no leather will be wasted. However, you also have to avoid bad spots in the leather.

When using medium weight leather, the patterns can be laid out without regard to grain. On light weight leather and fur skins the patterns should be laid out with the grain, the grain being the run of the leather from the head to the tail. Leather stretches less lengthwise than it does from side to side; therefore, cutting the leather in accordance with the grain will help it to hang correctly. Whenever possible, lay a garment out the way the skin was on the animal.

Move the pattern around and try it from different angles so you get it in the right place, and then tape it down or glue it with all-purpose cement. When it is solidly in place, draw around the edges with a felt tip pen. Mark the holes for sewing or lacing by pricking the leather with an awl.

When the pattern is traced on the leather, lay the leather out on a flat wooden surface like a sheet of plywood. Holding your knife in a vertical position, push down and cut through the leather in a series of passes rather than trying to cut it all at once. Be careful not to cut the leather surrounding the patterns since you might wish to use it for another project. If the leather is light, use the scissors to cut it out because a knife tends to pull and stretch light leather.

The holes are punched with the revolving punch. The smallest size tube is used for punching holes for thread, rivets fit snugly in the holes punched by the medium tube and thongs take the largest size hole. The revolving punch will not punch holes in the interior of the pattern, so a drive punch is used to make the hole if a knife slit in the leather will not do the job.

The method of assembly or of joining the edges of the leather should be studied before the project begins. Fine sewn edges look well in a project such as a belt, while laced seams look best in knife sheaths and rifle scabbards. Some projects are riveted and brass rivets add a rich touch to brown leather. A holster, rugged belt, or gun sling is often riveted.

Seams are called "flat fell," "top stitched," "French," and "overcast." Some of the thread sewn stitches are "running stitch," "double running stitch," and "saddle stitch." The lace joints can be sewn with running stitch and the saddle stitch. Some articles won't be sewn, but they will be riveted or glued and riveted; many will be sewn, riveted, and even laced on the same project.

Making an item from leather goods is a step by step procedure much like assembling a kitchen stool from wood or making clothing from cloth. A good first project is a pair of chopper mittens. The pair described will be sized for an adult male, but the pattern can be cut down for children and women.

Making Leather Mittens

First the proper cut of leather should be selected. If you have a deerskin tanned it will make fine mittens. If the mittens will be used for chopping wood and such strenuous tasks, use the thickest part of

CHOPPER MITTEN PATTERN

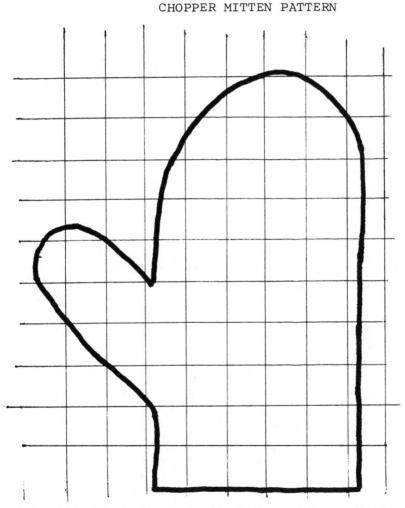

Make two patterns for each mitten. Use deerskin, elk skin, moosehide or cowhide that is chrome or vegetable tanned.

the thickest deerskin that you have. Always lay the pattern out so you cut from the head towards the tail with the grain of the leather so it will be the most resistant to tearing. After the pattern is selected but before you cut valuable leather, cut the mittens out from paper or cloth, baste the pieces together, and try them on. Although cardboard patterns are usually used, metal patterns are easier to mark around and are worth the time it takes to make them if the project will be repeated.

After the pattern work is completed, lay the skin on a flat surface at a comfortable working height with the flesh side up. The only time that leather patterns are laid out on the grain side is if the flesh side is too rough to make tracing lines. Each piece should have a pattern so it can be laid out to make the best possible use of the leather. Try the pattern several different ways until the straight lines lay against each other as much as possible. Avoid the cuts and abrasions in the hide, especially if the abrasions appear to weaken the skin.

If you are using a metal pattern, hold it firmly in place with one hand and cut around it with the other; if you have a paper pattern, draw lines around it, and then cut it out on the lines. The lines can be marked with soft pencil or magic marker, but the scratch awl is probably the most accurate instrument to use. If a mistake is made with a scratch awl the lines can be burnished out, but lines made with ink are very hard to remove from leather. Use a very sharp utility knife or a pair of scissors to cut the hide.

Now lay the pieces of the mittens grain side to grain side. Match them evenly, baste them together, and start sewing the seams together at the cuff; continue sewing around to the other cuff. If a sewing machine is not available, stitch them by hand using eight to ten stitches to the inch. Elastic can be sewn in at the cuff to make the mitten fit tighter at the wrist.

Making Indian Moccasins

The next project is a pair of Indian moccasins which will require about three to four square feet of unblemished leather, four feet of lacing, and twelve feet of strong string for sewing. The pattern shown fits a size ten foot. Use a ¾-inch grid for size six feet. To adjust the pattern for a different size foot, step on a sheet of paper and draw around the foot, holding the pencil vertically. After the complete tracing is made, draw another line the shape of the foot but ⅝ inch outside the first to allow for sewing and the sides of the moccasin.

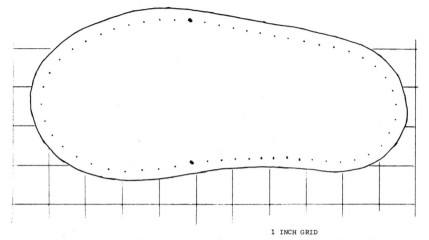

Make two sole sections for Indian moccasins, reversing one for the left foot. This pattern is a size ten.

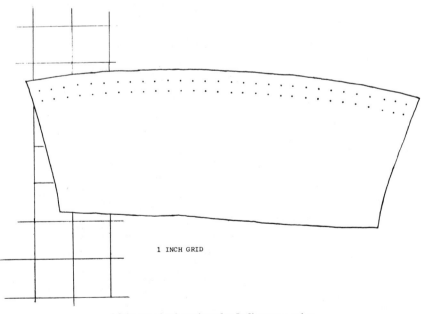

Make two heel sections for Indian moccasins.

Cut out both left and right sole patterns as well as two vamps and two heels so the entire pattern can be laid out on the leather before cutting starts to avoid wasting leather.

After the pieces are cut out, the sole is punched for sewing with each hole spaced ⅜ inch apart in a pattern ¼ inch inside the outer rim of the sole. The heel and vamp are punched for sewing with a double row of holes spaced ¼ inch apart.

You will need a two-inch needle and about four feet of sewing thread for each moccasin. Start by sewing from the inside of the moccasin through the fourth hole in the vamp as shown. Pull the thread to

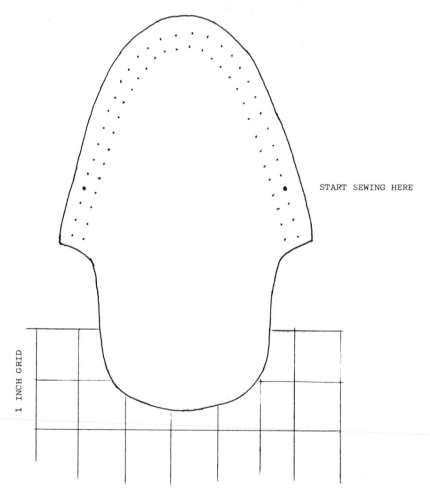

START SEWING HERE

1 INCH GRID

Make two vamp sections for Indian moccasins.

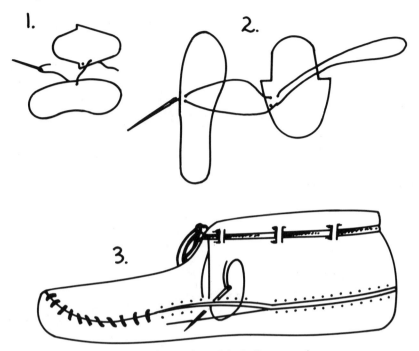

Stitching the sections of the Indian moccasin.

the outside, but leave about 3½ inches of thread inside the boot. Then insert the needle through the same hole in the top row and to the next forward lower hole in the bottom row of the vamp, then through the hole in the sole.

Continue to sew like this around the bottom to the fourth hole before the end, and then insert the heel and sew it around as shown in the drawing. When the last holes are reached, take the end of the thread from the needle and tie it to the end of the thread left when the sewing was started.

14

Solutions and Formulas

RELAXING FORMULAS FOR DRIED SKINS

1. Borax Solution
   1 ounce of borax, 1 gallon of warm water 90 to 100° F.
   Mix up enough to cover the skin, and soak three to five days for
   heavy skins. The longer it soaks the softer the flesh and tissue will
   be, but don't oversoak fur skins so the fur starts to slip. When
   soaking a thin fur skin, remove in four hours, or as soon as it is
   flexible.

2. Carbolic Acid Solution
   1 gallon water, 1½ tablespoons carbolic acid crystals
   Mix enough to cover a dried skin to relax it. If an extremely large
   skin must be relaxed, apply to the flesh side by brushing it on.

3. Water And Household Bleach
   1 ounce household bleach, 8 gallons water
   Use this formula for salted, dried, fur skins. Bleach retards bac-
   terial action which might cause hair loosening.

4. Water And Household Bleach
   1 teaspoon household bleach, 5 quarts of water
   Same formula as #3 but for a small skin.

5. Water, Household Bleach, and Ammonia
   1 ounce household bleach, 8 gallons water, 1 ounce ammonia
   Use this formula for dried, unsalted fur skins.

5A. 4 ounces of salt, 2 ounces Tide or liquid Ivory, 1 gallon of water

DEHAIRING SOLUTIONS

6. 1 gallon of soft water for each pound of skin
   Deerskin is sometimes soaked in clear water to loosen the hair.
   Although it is time consuming and there is a putrid odor, it elim-
   inates the bating step when skin is being tanned under primitive
   conditions. Skin condition can be adversely affected.

7. 1 gallon of hardwood ashes, 1 gallon of caustic (common) lime, 5
   gallons of warm water
   Soak the skin until the hair slips easily. (About five days.)

8. ¼ cup lye, 10 gallons warm water
   Dissolve lye in water. Wait until it cools then immerse skins and
   soak for two days or until the hair loosens, stirring frequently.

9. 3 pounds of caustic lime, 10 gallons of water
   Stir the lime in the water until it is completely dissolved, then soak
   the skins until the hair loosens. This can take up to ten days in
   cool weather.

DELIMING SOLUTIONS

10. 1 ounce lactic acid, 10 gallons water
    Immerse the rinsed skin and soak for twelve hours.

11. 1 pint white vinegar, 10 gallons water
    Same as #10.

12. 1 ounce acetic acid, 10 gallons water
    Same as #10.

13. 1 ounce ammonium sulfate crystals, 10 gallons of water
    Same as #10.

14. 1 ounce boric acid, 10 gallons of water
    Same as #10.

ACID TANNING SOLUTIONS

Caution: Wear eye and skin protection when using acids. Hides
tanned in these solutions cannot be tested by boiling. Don't
put acid in metal containers. Dispose of all acid solutions
in a safe place.

15. Oxalic Acid Tan
    2 ounces of oxalic acid, 2 cups of salt, 1 gallon warm soft water
    For small animal skins. Soak twenty-four hours.

16. Oxalic Acid Pickle Tan
    1 ounce oxalic acid, 14 ounces salt, 1 gallon water
    Immerse and soak for twelve to twenty-four hours, stirring once
    each eight hours. Oversoaking will not harm the skin.

16A. Vinegar Pickling Formula
    2 quarts of water, 2 quarts of white vinegar, 1 pound of salt

17. Sulfuric Acid Paste Tan
    ½ ounce pure, sulfuric acid or 1½ ounces automotive sulfuric acid,
    1 pound of salt
    Add enough water to make a paste, and spread it on the flesh side
    of a skin. Cover with sheet plastic and let stand six hours. Scrape
    off old paste and apply a new layer, leaving it uncovered to dry.

18. Sulfuric Acid Immersion Tan
    4 ounces automotive sulfuric acid for each pound of skin, 1 pound
    of salt, 1 gallon of water
    Immerse the fleshed skins and soak for three days, stirring often.

19. Sulfuric Acid Quick Tan
    3 cups of salt, 2 ounces of saltpeter, 1 ounce of borax, 1 gallon of
    warm, soft water, 1½ pints of automotive-type sulfuric acid
    A strong solution that can tan a small skin in three hours or even
    less. Neutralize with bicarbonate of soda.

20. Acid-Alum Tan

For every pound of skin use: 1½ tablespoons of carbolic acid crystals, ½ pound of salt, ¼ pound of alum, 1 gallon of water

Soak a skin for up to six days until the tanning color has fully penetrated the skin.

21. Acid-Oil Tan

Dissolve ¼ pound salt in ½ gallon water. Add 1 ounce thirty-three percent sulfuric acid.

Spread the skin out, hair side down and use a paint brush to apply this solution to the flesh side. Sprinkle a layer of sawdust over the skin, cover with a thin sheet of plastic, and let stand twelve hours. Scrape off the sawdust and apply a coating of fifty percent neat's-foot oil and warm water. Stretch the skin until dry and dampen with a solution of one gallon of water and 1½ tablespoons carbolic acid. Roll up until the skin is relaxed, then beam until soft.

ALUM TANNING SOLUTION

Caution: Alum is caustic. Do not take internally.

22. Alum Tans

Dissolve 1 pound of alum in 1 gallon of water. In another container dissolve 4 ounces of washing soda and 1 cup of salt in ½ gallon of soft water.

Very slowly pour the soda-salt solution into the alum solution and stir it well. Immerse the skin, stirring frequently. Small skins will tan in forty-eight hours, larger skins in three to four days. After tanning, soak in borax solution for one hour and then rinse well.

23. Alum Paste Tan

Mix together 2 ounces washing soda, 4 ounces salt, 8 ounces ammonium or potassium alum

Add enough soft water to make a paste. Apply to the flesh side of a skin and cover so it doesn't dry out. Leave for three days, scrape off, and apply a fresh coat. Repeat three more times; then rinse well with borax water.

24. Alum and Sour Milk Tan

Combine 2½ pounds of alum, 1 pound of salt, and 1 pound of oatmeal

Mix well and add enough sour milk to make a thin paste. Apply

the paste to the flesh side of the skin, making sure it stays moist.
Requires a minimum of twenty-four hours to complete a tan.

25. Alum and Bran Tan
    Warm 1 gallon of soft water to 120° F. and add 4 cups of bran.
    Allow to stand in a warm room for forty-eight hours or until it
    ferments; then heat to almost boiling and add 1 cup of salt. Cool
    and add 1 pound of alum. When lukewarm, immerse the skins in
    the wet bran. Let stand thirty-six to forty-eight hours, then rinse
    and beam.

26. Fresh Skin Tan
    Wash the blood and dirt from a fresh skin and spread it out to dry.
    When it reaches the damp stage, rub the following mixture on the
    skin: 2 parts salt, 1 part saltpeter, 1 part alum, 1 part bicarbonate
    of soda.
    Knead this mixture well into the skin and roll the skin up or place
    it in an oversized plastic bag so it doesn't dry and let it stand with
    one end inclined so any fluid can run out for two weeks. Unroll,
    flesh away all fat and membrane, swab with tanning oil, and beam
    until soft. Works best with rabbit skins.

27. Dry-Curing Formula
    1 quart salt, 1 pound alum, ¼ pound saltpeter
    Rub into well-fleshed skins.

28. Salt Alum Solution
    5 pounds salt, 2 pounds alum, 10 gallons water
    Use for an immersion tan.

29. Combination Solution
    1 pound aluminum sulfate or potassium alum, 1 pound of salt, 3
    ounces of gambier

30. Tawing Paste With Fat Liquor
    Use this formula for fur skins that are naturally dry or skins that
    have been degreased because of too much grease or odor. Egg yolk
    is one of the few oils that is naturally soluble in water and thus is
    absorbed into the skin.
    12 ounces of potash alum, 6 ounces of salt, 8 ounces of egg yolk,
    2 quarts of soft water
    Heat water to almost boiling, stirring in alum and salt until it is

dissolved. Beat the egg yolks and blend into the alum and salt solution, then take one third of the mixture and mix with enough wheat flour to make a moderately thick paste. Pour the paste down the center of flesh side of the skin and spread out to the belly area with a brush, covering entire skin with an even coat. Skin must be damp but not wet. Keep the tannage from drying out by covering it with plastic or newspaper. In six hours apply a fresh coat and another six hours later. Let the final coat stay on for thirty-six hours. By this time the skin should be white all the way through, if it isn't, cover again and let it stand overnight.

CHROME TANNING SOLUTIONS

Caution: Chrome crystals are poisonous. Use eye and skin protection when handling them. Don't use a metal container.

This solution produces the most durable leather. It is permanent since it won't leach out in water. It stains the skin a blue-green color.

31. Chrome Powder Tanning Formula
    Weigh the skin and for each pound of skin use: 1 gallon water, 8 ounces salt
    Soak the fleshed, pickled skin in this solution for one half hour. Remove the skin, and pour in one half of the following solution. For every pound of skin, mix 1 quart of warm (120° F.) water with 3 ounces of chrome crystals.
    When this is mixed, remove the skin from the salt solution, pour half the chrome solution in the salt, stir well, and replace the skin. Leave skin in this solution for twelve hours, then remove the skin and add the rest of the chrome tannage. Replace the skin and let it soak for four to five days, stirring it often. When it is tanned, the chrome color will penetrate the skin and it will pass the boiling test. Neutralize with baking soda (formula #38).

32. Chrome Crystals and Sodium Carbonate Formula
    Weigh the skin and for each pound of skin use: ¾ ounce sodium carbonate, 1½ ounces salt, ½ gallon of water
    Mix the salt and soda in the water until it is dissolved. In another container for each pound of skin, mix: 1½ ounces of pure chrome alum ($K_2 SO_4$, $Cr_2(SO_4)_3$,$24H_2O$) crystals, 3 quarts of water
    Combine the two solutions, stirring it very well to be sure all

ingredients are combined and dissolved. Let this set for forty-eight hours before it is used, then pour half the solution in a container, stir it well, and immerse the skin. Let soak for two days stirring it well. After two days, remove the skin, add the rest of the solution, stir well, and replace the skin. Let soak for another two to three days. Then test for complete color penetration of the skin. If penetration isn't complete, return skin to tanning solution for forty-eight hours. Neutralize with baking soda.

33. Chrome Tan For Snake Skin
    1 gallon water, 3 ounces salt, ½ ounce chromium potassium sulfate

VEGETABLE TANNING SOLUTIONS

Caution: Don't use metal containers.

34. For Each Pound Of Skin:
    5 ounces of gambier, 1 ounce of salt, 1 gallon of water

35. For Each Pound Of Skin:
    4 ounces of sumac extract, 1 ounce salt, 1 gallon of water

36. For Each Pound Of Skin:
    5 ounces of Tannin-Blend, 1 ounce salt, 1 gallon of water

37. For Each Pound Of Skin:
    16 ounces of ground oak or hemlock bark, 1 ounce of salt, 1 gallon of water
    Simmer bark in water for three hours or steep in warm water for forty-eight hours.

All the vegetable tanning agents are dissolved in boiling water and then added to the salt and water after it cools. When ground bark is used, the solution should stand a minimum of forty-eight hours to steep and the bark can be left in the water or strained out. For all vegetable tans, keep the acidity about 4.5 to 5. If it gets too acidic, adjust the pH by adding small amounts of bicarbonate of soda, using pH indicator papers to check the acidity. Stir and work the skins as they are tanning. Light skins tan in three to five days and heavy skins in five to fourteen days. After the tanning solution has completely penetrated the skin, remove it from the tannage, rinse well, and oil and stake it as needed.
Quicker results will be obtained if the skin is pickled with sulfuric acid

or oxalic acid or pretanned with alum before the vegetable tan. However, very good results can be obtained without pickling. Be sure to raise the pH of the pickled skin to between 4.5 and 5 before vegetable tanning.

NEUTRALIZING SOLUTIONS

38. 1 ounce bicarbonate of soda, 1 gallon of water
    Use this solution for neutralizing chrome tannage and acid solutions.

39. 1 ounce boric acid, 1 gallon warm water
    Neutralizes alkaline solutions.

40. 4 ounces borax, 1 gallon water
    Neutralizes acid.

41. 2 ounces of calcium carbonate, 1 gallon water
    For neutralizing acid.

DEGREASING SOLUTIONS

Caution: Skins should be partially dried before degreasing, as water will prevent the solvents from working properly. Use extreme caution when using these flammable solutions.

42. 4 tablespoons of Tide or liquid Ivory, 1 gallon of warm water
    Wash and soak the skins in the water for ten to fifteen minutes. This will work best for skins with light grease; however, several baths with drying periods between them will degrease most skins.

43. 5 gallons full strength kerosene
    Work and soak skin until grease is dissolved, then remove and wash in one ounce of household detergent to each gallon of warm water. Rinse well and dry quickly.

44. 5 gallons white gasoline
    Work and soak the skin for fifteen minutes. Remove and tumble or coat with sawdust, powdered chalk, or kitty litter.

45. 4 gallons white gasoline, 1 gallon alcohol
    Work and soak the skin for ten to fifteen minutes. The skin can then be washed in one ounce of household detergent to each gallon

of water or coated with sawdust and beaten to remove the sawdust containing the grease and dirt. If the skin is free of dirt before starting the degreasing process, it doesn't have to be washed.

46. Chlorinated hydrocarbons (dry cleaning fluid)
    Either immerse skin or saturate a rag and wipe the skin.
    Some skins must be deodorized with the degreasing formula. In this case detergents will not give good results. Gasoline, kerosene, and dry cleaning fluids will deodorize, and this is needed for bear, skunk, and goat skins, among others.
    Caution: Extremely flammable. Use outside if possible.

FAT-LIQUORING FORMULAS

47. 1 pint warm, soft water, 1 pint sulfonated neat's-foot oil or sulfonated castor oil
    Sulfonated oil is partially soluble in water. Many other commercial tanning oils are available from tanning supply outlets, and they will not stain skins.

48. 1 cup sulfonated neat's-foot oil, 1 cup nonsulfonated neat's-foot oil
    This will discolor some skins.

49. 1 cup neat's-foot oil, cod-liver, or castor oil, 1 cup melted beef or mutton tallow
    Combine the two by heating the tallow until it is liquid. When it cools it will be a soft paste. Increase the oil to make a softer mixture, decrease to make a harder paste. This is commonly called dubbin which can discolor some skins.

50. 1 pound bear or raccoon fat heated to the liquid stage, 1 pint #10 nondetergent engine oil
    Mix together. This mixture will stain some skins tanned by some processes. Try a small piece first before committing the entire skin to this mixture.

51. 1 part cod-liver oil, 1 part neat's-foot oil or castor oil
    Might discolor some skins. Try it first if you want to retain the skin color.

52. 1 cup egg yolk, 5 cups warm water
Separate the egg yolks from the whites and beat into warm water. Brush on the skin. Egg yolk is twenty percent fat and is one of the few oils naturally soluble in water. Does not stain or darken most skins.

Glossary

Acetic acid   A colorless, pungent liquid contained in vinegar which neutralizes alkali and pickles skins.

Acid   A sour substance which turns blue litmus paper red and reacts with alkalis to form salts. In tanning, sulfuric acid is the strongest acid commonly used and acetic acid is the mildest.

Alkali   Alkalis turn red litmus paper blue and have the ability to neutralize acids. Caustic soda is a strong alkali and ammonia is a weak alkali.

Alum   A common name applied to any of a series of double crystalline salts. Ammonium and potash alum are perhaps the most common forms and may be used interchangeably in tanning.

Aluminum sulfate   This substance is contained in alum and can be used as a tanning substance.

Baking soda   This substance is used to neutralize acids and is commonly called bicarbonate of soda.

Basicity   Term used to describe the tanning power of a chrome tanning salt.

Borax   A white crystalline compound used in tanning for a softening aid and a cleaning agent.

Boric acid   A white, crystalline, mildly acidic and antiseptic compound which can be used as a deliming agent.

190

Chemical tan   The process of tanning with alum or chrome.

Chrome   Chromium potassium sulfate, also called chrome alum, and an excellent tanning substance.

Cornmeal   Useful for cleaning furs and for absorbing grease after a skin is immersed in a degreasing liquid.

Degreasing   Immersing a skin in a degreasing solution to remove the natural fats when they would interfere with the tanning process or if they are odoriferous.

Dehair   To remove the hair from a skin that will be made into leather. This is usually done with an alkali bath.

Deliming   Soaking skins in a weak acid solution to neutralize lime or other alkalis.

Drumming   Tumbling skins in a drum to soften, oil, or dry them.

Dubbin   A mixture of liquid oils and tallow used for greasing and softening hides.

Fleshing   Removal of fat, flesh, and gristle which adheres to the skin.

Fleshing beam   A rounded working surface on which the hide is spread for fleshing.

Fleshing knife   A knife designed to scrape the hair, fat, and excess tissue off of the hide. The 15- to 17-inch blade is slightly curved and has a handle on each end.

Flesh side   The side of the skin that goes against the carcass.

Furs   Skins tanned with the hair on.

Gambier   A tanning and dyeing substance made from the leaves of a Malayan shrub.

Gasoline   Used for cleaning implements. White gasoline is used for degreasing.

Green skins   Untanned, fresh skins.

Hair slip   When the hair is loosened by decomposition of the skin.

Hydrated lime   The common form of lime that is used for dehairing skins. Also called calcium hydroxide or slaked lime.

Kerosene   Pure kerosene is used for degreasing.

Kip   The skins of smaller beef cattle or calves.

Neat's-foot oil   An animal oil used to soften and condition skins which is made by boiling cattle feet until the oil separates out.

Pelt   Animal skins with the fur or hair on. Usually refers to the dried skins of small furbearing animals.

Pickling   Treating skins and hides with salt and acid to preserve them.

Pumice   Can be used as an abrasive for thinning hides.

Rawhide   Untanned and dehaired animal skins prepared by stretching and dry curing.

Skinning knife   A slender, razor-sharp knife.

Skin pullers   Taxidermist's skin-pulling pliers that are useful for stretching skins as they dry.

Slicker   A slicker is a 5- or 6-inch wedge of metal or wood used to push water and oil out of a skin.

Slicking out   Scraping a leather surface to eliminate wrinkles and push out excess water and oil.

Staking   Working a tanned skin across the edge of a staking board to soften and smooth it.

Sulfonated oil   Oil treated so that it contains sulfonic acid and hence is partly soluble in water.

Sulfuric acid   A compound of hydrogen, sulfur, and oxygen that is used as a pickle and as a tanning solution. It is a very strong and corrosive acid, and extreme care should be taken when using it.

Tannic acid   The active principle in many vegetable substances which will convert a skin into leather.

Tawing   An old English term for treating skins with alum, especially when applied as a paste.

Washing soda   Sal soda is another name for this water softener and cleaning agent. It is a form of sodium carbonate.

Index

Acid, carbolic, 134
Acid, lactic, 49
Acid, oxalic, 17, 151
Acid, skin pickling, 50
Acid, sulfuric, 50, 103
Acid, tanning solutions, 182
Alkalis, ammonia, 4
Alkalis, washing soda, 4, 28
Alligator, description, 129
Alligator hide, fleshing, 132
Alligator hide, salting the hide, 132
Alligator hide, tanning, 132, 133
Alligator, skinning, 130
Alum, aluminum sulphate, 11, 24, 28
Alum, ammonium, 11, 28
Alum, potash, 11, 28
Alum, tanning solutions, 183
Ammonia, for soaking skins, 4
Antelope skins, 172

Bark, for dye, 53
Bark, for tanning thick leather, 125
Bark, hemlock, 11, 22
Bark, oak, 11, 22
Bark, sumac, 4
Bating, deerskin, 48
Bating, with vinegar, 5
Bear, field dressing, 87
Bear, hunting, 1, 7, 85, 97
Bear skin, chrome tanning, 94
Bear skin, degreasing, 94
Bear skin, drying the hair, 94
Bear skin, fleshing, 92
Bear skin, poisoning, 96
Bear skin, protecting, 91
Bear skin, rugs, 97
Bear skin, salting, 91
Bear skin, softening, 96
Bear skin, trimming, 96
Bear skin, washing, 93

Bear, skinning, 87–90
Beaver, description, 7, 18, 67
Beaver skin, degreasing, 72
Beaver skin, fleshing, 70, 71
Beaver skin, tanning, 72
Beaver, skinning 69
Beaver, trapping, 69
Bench, tanning bench construction, 148
Bird skin, as a trophy, 139
Bird skin, tanning, 141
Bird, skinning, 139
Breaking bench construction, 158
Breaking blade, 159
Buckskin, 42
Buckskin, from sheep skin, 107
Buckskin Indian style, 53
Buckskin, smoking, 55

Caribou, general information, 81
Chrome, 11
Chrome tanning, deerskins, 50
Chrome tanning, heavy leather, 126
Chrome tanning, solutions, 185
Coyote, description, 59, 60
Coyote skin, fleshing, 63
Coyote skin, softening, 64
Coyote skin, tanning, 63
Coyote, skinning, 60
Coyote, trapping, 60

Deer skin, bating, 48, 49
Deer skin, dyeing, 51
Deer skin, fleshing and dehairing, 47, 48
Deer skin, salting, 47
Deer skin, softening, 51
Deer skin, tanning, 49, 50
Deer skin, weight, 50
Deer skinning, 42
Deer skins, needed for clothing, 43

Degreasing, agents, 7
Degreasing, solutions, 187
Degreasing, why it's done, 7
Degreasing, with dry cleaning fluids, gasoline, kerosene, 7
Dehairing a skin, 5
Dehairing, solutions, 181
Dehairing, tools, 5
Deliming, solutions, 181
Detergent, 81
Domestic, animal skins, 115
Domestic, hair on tanning, 121
Domestic, immersion tanning, 121
Domestic, paste tanning, 121
Domestic, preparing to tan, 116
Domestic skin, fleshing, 118
Domestic skin price, 115
Domestic skin, salting, cow hide, 118
Domestic skin, tanning supplies and equipment, 116
Dubbin, 23

Egg white, 24
Elk, general information, 81

Fat liquoring formula, 188, 189
Fish skin, descaling, 134
Fish skin, salting and fleshing, 133
Fish, skinning, 133
Fisher, 65
Fleshing, aids, 4
Fleshing, beams, 8, 9
Fleshing, beam construction, 150
Fleshing, for the novice, 4
Fleshing, fresh skins, 4
Fleshing, knives, 8
Fleshing, methods, 4
Fleshing, why it's done, 4
Fox, gray, 59
Fox, red, 56
Fox skin, fleshing, 59

Fox skin, tanning, 59
Fox, skinning, 58
Fox, trapping, 57
Fox, trapping, killing the fox, 58
Frame, skin stretching, 118, 128
Frogs, skin tanning, 138

Garbage can, 116
Gasoline, white, 128
Goats, general information, 108
Goat skin, bating, 110
Goat skin, degreasing, 110
Goat skin, fleshing, 110
Goat skin, tanning, 111
Goat, skinning, 108

Hares, general information, 40–41
Heavy leather, oil tanning, 127
Heavy leather, tanning, 123, 129
Heavy leather, uses, 124, 128
Hide, freezing, 2
Hide, "green," 16
Hide, salting, 2
Hide, stretching, 3
Hide, washing, 2, 4

Indian, moccassins, 176
Indian, tanning, 162

Kitty litter, 79, 113
Knife, construction, 143–148
Knife, sharpening stone, 147
Knife, skivving, 77
Knives, fleshing, 8

Leather, grading, 169, 171
Leather, "kips," 171
Leather mittens, 175
Leather, moccassins, 176

Leather, patterns, 172
Leather, projects, 172
Leather, sides, 171
Leather, sewing, 174
Leather, working tools, 172
Leaves, alfalfa 12
Leaves, tea, 11
Leaves, willow, 4
Lime, deliming, 11, 21
Lizards, skin tanning, 138

Machinery, for home tanning, 10,
    103–104
Mink skin, finishing, 40
Mink skin, fleshing, 39
Mink skin, tanning, 39, 40
Mink, skinning, 38
Moose, general information, 81
Moose skin, cleaning, 76, 79
Moose skin, fat liquoring, 83
Moose skin, finishing, 78, 83
Moose skin, fleshing, 79
Moose skin, hair on tanning, 77
Moose skin, Kwik-Tan process, 78
Moose skin, pulling, staking and
    tumbling, 84
Moose skin, salting the skin, 75
Moose skin, tanning for leather, 79
Moose skin, tanning combination,
    81
Moose skin, thinning, 77
Moose skin, weight, 76
Muskrat, general information, 24
Muskrat skin, container, 167
Muskrat skin, fleshing and
    stretching, 27, 28
Muskrat skin, tanning or tawing
    the skin, 28
Muskrat skinning, 25–27
Muskrat, trapping, 25

Naptha, 128
Neat's Foot Oil, 30, 36, 114, 128
Neutralizing solutions, 187

Oil, cod liver, 128
Otter, 65
Otter skin, fleshing, 65
Otter skin, relaxing, 66
Otter skin, tanning, 66
Otter, trapping, 65

Pelt, what it is, 4
Pig skin, dehairing, 113
Pig skin, dyeing, 114
Pig skin, fleshing, 113
Pig skin, softening, 114
Pig skin, tanning, 114
Pig skinning, 111, 112
Plastic bag, for apron, 48
Plastic bag, garbage can, 8
Plastic bag, garbage pails, 20
Plastic, sheeting, 49, 123
Plumbers plunger, 81
Poultice tanning, 167
Primitive tanning, 162, 164

Rabbits, general information,
    40–41
Rabbit skin, tanning, 41
Rabbit, skinning, 41
Raccoon skin, dehairing, 21
Raccoon skin, finishing, 23
Raccoon skin, fleshing, 19, 20
Raccoon skin, leather, 22
Raccoon skin, salting, 20
Raccoon skin, skinning, 19
Raccoon skin, stretching, 19
Raccoon, tanning, 74
Raccoon, trapping, 18, 19
Rawhide, from skins, 165
Rawhide, laces, 165
Rawhide, products, 166
Rawhide, uses in early America,
    164, 165
Relaxing formulas, 180–181
Reptile skins, 129
Rubber gloves, 127

Safety, 10
Salt, type used in tanning, 91
Salting a hide, 2, 3, 118
Sandpaper for softening a skin, 18
Sawdust, 126
Sawdust and cornmeal for cleaning
    fur, 18, 37
Sewing, leather, 179
Sheep, 100
Sheep, shearing, 103
Sheep skin, cleaning, 101
Sheep skin, dry cleaning, 104
Sheep skin, fleshing, 101
Sheep skin, rinsing, 104
Sheep skin, tanning, 102–105
Sheep skin, tawing tan, 102
Sheep skin, washing, 103
Sheep, skinning, 100
Skin and hair slippage, 314
Skin bag from a muskrat, 167
Skin, choosing a good skin, 2
Skin, damage 7
Skin, defects, 4
Skin, dirty, 4
Skin, salt water bath, 3
Skin, soaking, 3
Skin, spoilage, 2
Skin, stiff, 3
Skin, thickness and weight, 169
Skinning, case skinning, 2
Skinning, holes in skins, 4
Skinning, large animals, 2
Skinning, open skinning, 1
Skinning, proper time, 1
Skinning, small animals, 2
Skinning, squirrel skinning, 14
Skunk skin, degreasing, 35
Skunk skin, finishing, 36, 37
Skunk, fleshing, 35
Skunk, skinning, 33
Skunk, trapping, 33
Slicker, 30, 126
Slicker, construction, 156
Snake skin, 137
Snake skin, descaling, 137
Snake skin, tanning, 138

Snake, skinning, 137
Soda, bicarbonate, 127
Softening skins, 7–9
Splits, leather, 171
Stake, construction, 156
Staking boards, 9
Staking methods, 9
Squirrels, 13, 14
Squirrel skin, 13, 14
Squirrel skin, finishing, 17, 18
Squirrel skin, fleshing, 15, 16
Squirrel skin, rinsing, 17
Squirrel skin, tanning, 17
Squirrel skin, washing, 15
Squirrel, skinning, 14, 15

Tanning, baths, 5
Tanning, boiling test, 6, 51
Tanning, chemicals, 5, 6
Tanning containers, 8
Tanning, first project, 13
Tanning, general procedures, 1
Tanning history, Egyptian leather,
 160
Tanning history, August Schultz,
 161
Tanning, oil, 7, 79
Tanning, room, 8
Tanning skins, alligators, 129
Tanning skins, bear, 85
Tanning skins, beaver, 67
Tanning skins, coyote, 59
Tanning skins, cowhide, 120
Tanning skins, deer, 49
Tanning skins, elk, 75
Tanning skins, fox, 56
Tanning skins, goat, 108
Tanning skins, horsehides, 118

Tanning skins, mink, 38
Tanning skin, moose, 75
Tanning skins, muskrat, 24
Tanning skins, sheep, 100
Tanning skins, skunk, 33
Tanning skins, snake, 137
Tanning skins, squirrel, 13
Tanning skins, weasel, 31
Tanning solutions, 182–187
Tanning, vegetable solutions, 6
Tanning, water, 8
Tawing, paste, 28
Tools, leather working 172
Tools, tanning, 143
Traps, beaver, 67, 69
Traps, coyote, 60
Traps, fox, 57
Traps, live, 25
Traps, mink, 57
Traps, skunk, 33
Traps, steel, 57
Traps, weasel, 3

Vacuum cleaner, 18
Vegetable tanning solutions, 186
Vinegar, 127

Water, rain, 9
Water, tap, 9
Weasel, fur, 31
Weasel, skinning, 32
Weasel, tanning, 33
Weasel, trapping, 31, 32
Wood, barrel, 115
Wood, wedges, 8, 44
Wool, 107